THE FORGOTTEN TUDOR WOMEN

ANNE SEYMOUR, JANE DUDLEY & ELISABETH PARR

Facebook page:

www.facebook.com/theforgottentudorwomen

Twitter:

https://twitter.com/SylviaBSo

Editorial services: Jennifer Quinlan

http://historicaleditorial.blogspot.com/

ISBN: 978172

This book is dedicated to my daughter, Amanda, who makes me proud every day.

Contents

Prologue: The Forgotten Tudor Women 1

Family trees 3

Chapter 1: Lady-in-waiting 6

Chapter 2: The Queen's sister-in-law 19

Chapter 3: Brush with treason 39

Chapter 4: Scandals and rivalries 47

Chapter 5: Queen in all but name 84

Chapter 6: Shadow of the Tower 91

Chapter 7: The Dudleys ascendant 133

Chapter 8: Reversal of fortune 142

Chapter 9: In and out of royal favour 175

Chapter 10: In high favour with the Queen 181

Chapter 11: Mother of the traitor 198

Chapter 12: Death of a marchioness 216

Chapter 13: This tedious suit 225

Chapter 14: The duchess's last years 239

Chapter 15: Setting all things in order 250

Appendix 1: When was Anne Seymour born? 268

Appendix 2: The children of Anne and Edward Seymour 269

Picture section 276

Selected Bibliography 293

PROLOGUE: THE FORGOTTEN TUDOR WOMEN

Edward Seymour, Duke of Somerset. John Dudley, Duke of Northumberland. William Parr, Marquis of Northampton.

These three men and their political careers are described in detail in historical books. Their wives, on the other hand, are often confined to the footnotes of history. Yet Anne Seymour, Jane Dudley and Elisabeth Parr all have their own unique stories to tell. Born into the most turbulent period of England's history, these women's lives interplayed with the great dramas of the Tudor age, and their stories deserve to be told independently of their husbands. Yet, as has been noted by earlier historians, writing the history of Tudor women is no easy task: "Women's lives from the sixteenth century can rarely be constructed except when these women have had influential connections with notable men."[1]

Anne Seymour served all of Henry VIII's six wives and brushed with treason more than once, but she died in her bed as a wealthy old matriarch. Jane Dudley was a wife and mother who fought for her family until her last breath. Elisabeth Parr, sister-in-law of Queen Katherine Parr, married for love and became Elizabeth I's favourite lady-in-waiting.

The Tudor age was a hazardous time for ambitious women: courtly life exposed them to "pride, envy, indignation, scorning and derision", beheadings were part of everyday life, death in childbirth was a real possibility and plagues sweeping regularly through the country could wipe out entire generations of families.[2] Yet Anne, Jane and Elisabeth lived through all this and left their indelible marks on history. It's high time for these women's stories to be heard.

NOTES

[1] Carol De Witte Bowles, *Women of the Tudor Court, 1501-1568*, p. 3.
[2] Muriel St Clare Byrne, *The Lisle Letters*, Volume 4, p 152.

FAMILY TREES

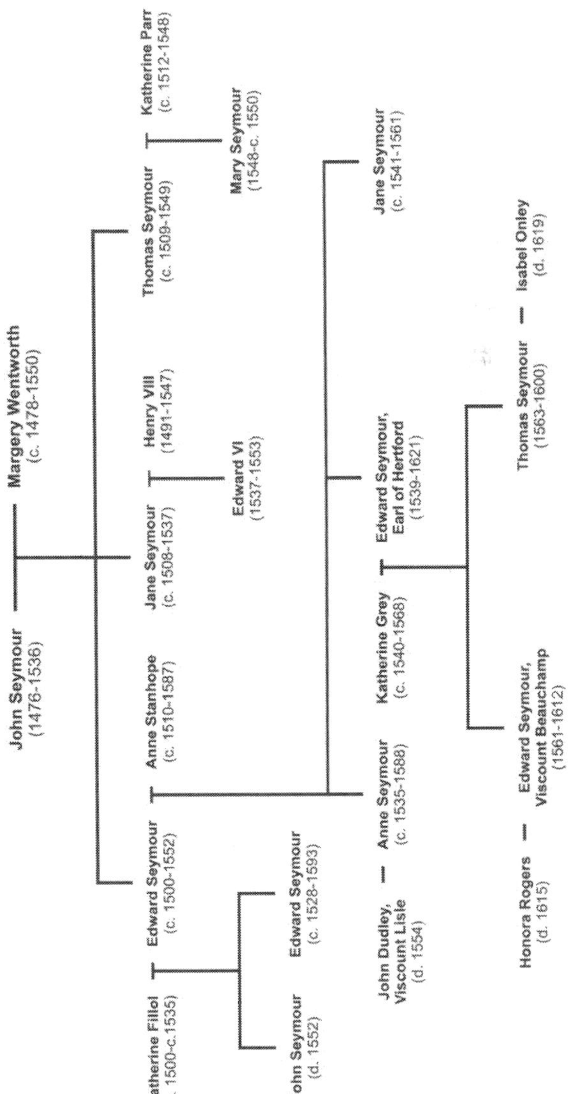

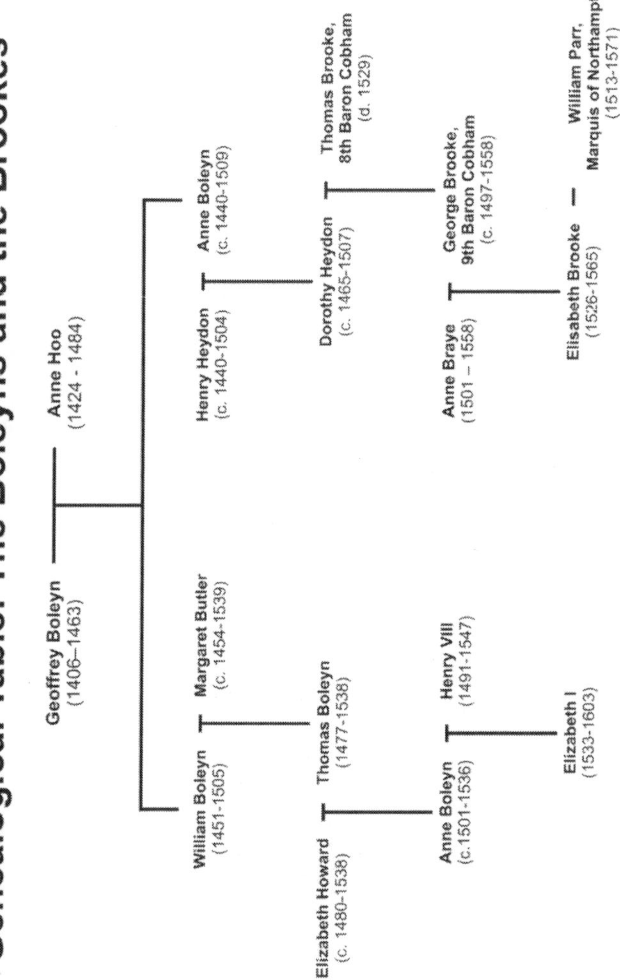
Genealogical Table: The Boleyns and the Brookes
Geoffrey Boleyn (1406–1463)
Anne Hoo (1424 - 1484)
William Boleyn (1451-1505)
Margaret Butler (c. 1454-1539)
Henry Heydon (c. 1440-1504)
Anne Boleyn (c. 1440-1509)
Elizabeth Howard (c. 1480-1538)
Thomas Boleyn (1477-1538)
Dorothy Heydon (c. 1465-1507)
Thomas Brooke, 8th Baron Cobham (d. 1529)
Anne Boleyn (c.1501-1536)
Henry VIII (1491-1547)
Anne Braye (1501 – 1558)
George Brooke, 9th Baron Cobham (c. 1497-1558)
Elizabeth I (1533-1603)
Elisabeth Brooke (1526-1565)
William Parr, Marquis of Northampton (1513-1571)

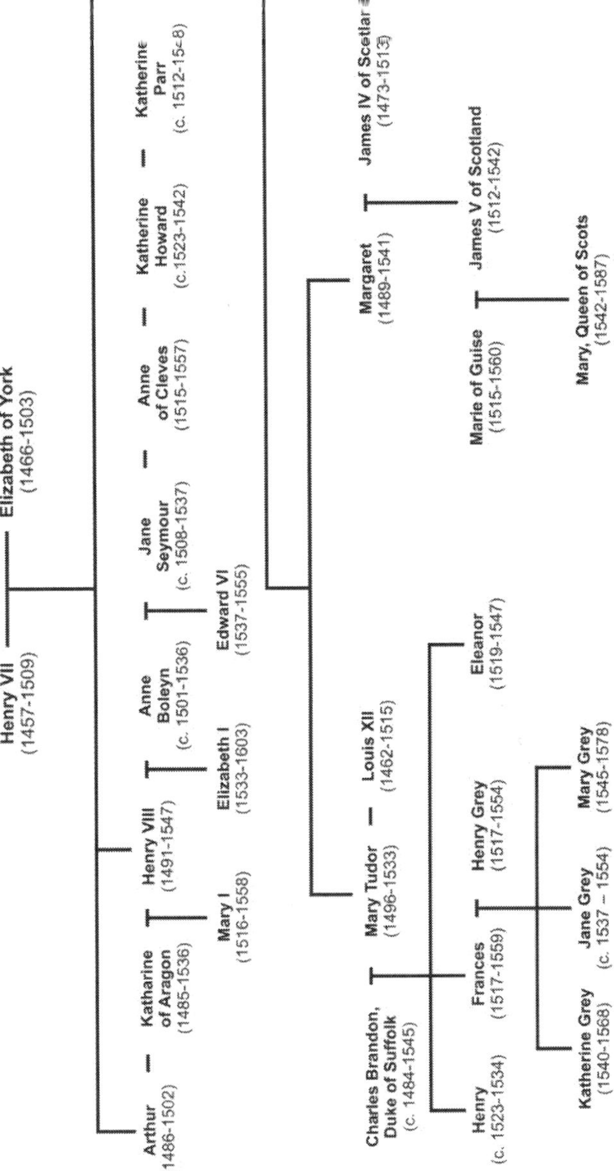
Genealogical Table: Henry VIII and His Family
Henry VII
(1457-1509)
Elizabeth of York
(1466-1503)
Arthur
(1486-1502)
Katharine of Aragon
(1485-1536)
Henry VIII
(1491-1547)
Anne Boleyn
(c. 1501-1536)
Jane Seymour
(c. 1508-1537)
Anne of Cleves
(1515-1557)
Katherine Howard
(c.1523-1542)
Katherine Parr
(c. 1512-1548)
Mary I
(1516-1558)
Elizabeth I
(1533-1603)
Edward VI
(1537-1555)
Mary Tudor
(1496-1533)
Louis XII
(1462-1515)
Margaret
(1489-1541)
James IV of Scotland
(1473-1513)
Charles Brandon, Duke of Suffolk
(c. 1484-1545)
Henry
(c. 1523-1534)
Frances
(1517-1559)
Henry Grey
(1517-1554)
Eleanor
(1519-1547)
Marie of Guise
(1515-1560)
James V of Scotland
(1512-1542)
Katherine Grey
(1540-1568)
Jane Grey
(c. 1537 – 1554)
Mary Grey
(1545-1578)
Mary, Queen of Scots
(1542-1587)

Chapter 1: Lady-in-Waiting

The court was the place to be for any noblewoman who wished to carve out a successful career in royal service and find an eligible husband. Anne Stanhope, born in 1510 to Sir Edward Stanhope and Elizabeth Bourchier, joined the household of Henry VIII's first wife, Katharine of Aragon, at some point after she reached her sixteenth year, the minimum age required to become a maid of honour.[1] She was well-positioned to become the Queen's maid—her father fought for Henry VII at the Battle of Stoke Field in 1487 and helped quash the Cornish Rebellion of 1497, after which he received a knighthood. Sir Edward died when Anne was an infant, but her mother remarried; her second husband was Sir Richard Page, a member of Henry VIII's Privy Chamber and a seasoned courtier.

The Queen's ladies were required by oath to be loyal to their royal mistress, and they received regular wages and livery that signalled their membership in her household. Materials used for livery gowns for the female servants throughout the entire reign of Henry VIII were usually damasks, velvets and satins, often russet in colour, trimmed with various furs depending on the wearer's social status. One of the most important perquisites was the "bouche of court", the right to receive food, drink and day-to-day materials according to one's rank.

As a maid of honour, Anne Stanhope was entitled to receive breakfasts and suppers as well as candles and timber for her fireplace. Anne would not have the luxury of a private chamber at court—privacy being a rare commodity at the Tudor court—but she shared a room and sometimes even a bed with other maids. Serving the Queen required waking up early in the morning and being ready for her every beck and call.

Katharine of Aragon was an accomplished princess who spoke fluent Flemish, French and English. She was very religious, rising each midnight to be present at matins and waking up early to attend morning prayers. She prayed on her knees without cushions and wore a penitential hair shirt beneath her opulent clothes made of luxurious materials imported from Spain, France, Italy and the Netherlands. Life within Katharine's household has often been characterised as dull, but there was nothing dull about the Queen's lifestyle. Her piety deepened as she grew older, but her love of finery and entertainment was still there: she employed her own minstrels and enjoyed watching masques and dances performed in her chambers.

By 1527, Henry VIII, the second Tudor monarch, had no male heir despite being married to Katharine of Aragon for eighteen years. The royal couple had only one surviving child, Princess Mary, who was born on 18 February 1516. The Queen, who reached her forty-second birthday on 16 December 1527, was deemed unable to bring forth any more children. The King, six years younger than his wife, was still in his prime, but without a legitimate heir to succeed him, he felt cursed. The biblical book of Leviticus forbade a man to marry his brother's widow, and Katharine of Aragon was briefly married to the King's elder brother, Arthur, who died in 1501. When Henry married Katharine in 1509, two months after his accession, he believed Katharine's assurances that after six months of marriage to Arthur she was still a virgin. But eighteen years and six pregnancies later, the King came to the startling conclusion that his marriage was cursed: "If a man shall take his brother's wife, it is an unclean thing . . . he shall be childless" (Leviticus 20: 21). Having a daughter instead of a son was as good as having no heirs at all in Henry VIII's view. In the spring of 1527, he set in motion his "great matter", as the King's divorce case was referred to in its early stages

Henry VIII's decision to repudiate Katharine of Aragon coincided with his infatuation with one of the Queen's maids of honour, Anne Boleyn. Daughter of Sir Thomas Boleyn and Elizabeth Howard, Anne was related to the earls of Ormond and dukes of Norfolk. Brought up at the French court since 1514, she was not among the most beautiful ladies of Henry VIII's court, but she was certainly one of the best educated. She caught the King's attention when she was first placed in the Queen's service in 1522 and intrigued him when she refused to become his mistress in 1526. The infatuated King tried to convince Mistress Boleyn to give in to his advances, but she stood her ground, hoping, perhaps, that Henry would grow tired of pursuing her. Yet the King's infatuation turned into obsession, and he decided to make Anne Boleyn his next wife.

By December 1528, Anne was well ensconced in the King's affections and recognized as Queen in all but name. The French ambassador remarked that "greater court is now paid to her every day than has been to the Queen for a long time".[2] Katharine of Aragon was highly popular among the King's subjects. She was perceived as the wronged wife of a philandering husband who paraded publicly with his royal mistress and had the audacity to claim his motives for divorce were pure. The Queen's ladies-in-waiting and maids of honour were quick to defend their royal mistress's honour and said that Anne Boleyn "so enticed the King, and brought him in such amours, that only for her sake and occasion he would be divorced from his Queen".[3]

Mistress Boleyn had many enemies at court. Chief among them was Cardinal Thomas Wolsey, Henry VIII's chief advisor. Boleyn hated Wolsey for breaking up her match with Henry Percy, heir of the Earl of Northumberland, in the early 1520s. At the beginning of the King's infatuation with Anne, Wolsey assisted Henry in the divorce case but hoped that the King would eventually grow tired of his mistress. This did not happen, and after the disastrous Blackfriars trial of 1529, when Katharine of Aragon triumphed over the King, Wolsey was in disgrace. Anne Boleyn and her allies convinced the King that the cardinal "has not done as much as he could have done to promote the marriage".[4]

On 9 October 1529, he was accused of praemunire—favouring the papal authority over the royal supremacy—and sent away from court in disgrace. On 18 October, the Dukes of Norfolk and Suffolk arrived at Wolsey's home in

York Palace and demanded the surrender of the Great Seal. On 26 October, Sir Thomas More filled Wolsey's post of Lord Chancellor. Wolsey had submissively retired from court in hope of softening the King's anger, surrendering his property into Henry's hands. Among the spoils was his episcopal palace in York, which later became known as Whitehall Palace.

In private, Wolsey attributed his fall from grace to that "serpentine enemy about the King". He meant, of course, Anne Boleyn, whom he had also dubbed "the Night Crow", referring, perhaps, to her dark colouring.[5] At the same time, however, the politically savvy cardinal was well aware that only Anne Boleyn was able to restore him to his former glory. Wolsey employed the help of his pupil Thomas Cromwell, the rising star of Henry VIII's court, who laboured on behalf of the disgraced cardinal. In one of his letters to Cromwell, Wolsey desperately wrote that "all possible means must be attempted for the attaining of her [Boleyn's] favour". Cromwell obliged and activated his contacts within the King's Privy Chamber. One of them was Sir Richard Page, Anne Stanhope's stepfather.

In May 1530, Cromwell informed Wolsey that "Mr Page received your letter directed unto my Lady Anne, and delivered the same. There is yet no answer. She gave kind words, but will not promise to speak to the King for you."[6] Wolsey was eventually pardoned, but his enemies still conspired against him. He died on 26 November 1530 on his way to the Tower of London.

By the 1530s, Henry VIII had grown tired of waiting for the pope's decision to annul his marriage and took matters into his own hands, declaring himself Head of the Church of England and issuing orders for the new Archbishop of Canterbury to nullify his unhappy match. When Katharine of Aragon was replaced by Anne Boleyn, Anne Stanhope joined Queen Anne's royal household in early 1534.[7] This turned out to be a great decision because, while serving at court, she met and married Sir Edward Seymour at some point in early 1535.

At the time of his marriage to Anne, Edward had been in royal service for twenty-one years. Born c. 1500 to Sir John Seymour and Margery Wentworth, he started his career in 1514 as a page to Henry VIII's younger sister, Mary Tudor, when she left England to marry Louis XII of France. In the 1520s he acquired the post of Master of the Horse in the household of the King's illegitimate son, Henry FitzRoy, and by 1531 he became an Esquire of the Body to Henry VIII, a prestigious post that required watching "day and night" over the King's person and helping him dress and undress.[8] Edward was among the King's servants when Henry VIII went to Calais in October 1532 to present Anne Boleyn as his future wife to Francis I, and in June 1533 he served as the Archbishop of Canterbury's carver during the banquet following the Queen's coronation.

Henry VIII's marriage to Anne Boleyn proved as fruitless as his union with Katharine of Aragon. Just like her banished predecessor, Anne gave birth to a healthy daughter but failed to produce sons. She gave birth to a stillborn child of an unknown sex in the summer of 1534 and miscarried a son on 29 January 1536, the day of Katharine of Aragon's funeral.

The King reverted to his old habit of taking mistresses early in his marriage to Anne, although none of them managed to keep his interest for long. This changed in 1536 when the King cast his fancy on one of Anne Stanhope's sisters-in-law, Jane Seymour. Jane's name first cropped up in Anne Boleyn's household in early 1534 when "Mistress Seymour" received a New Year's gift, but when Jane first came to the attention of the imperial ambassador in February 1536, she was described as a former servant of Katharine of Aragon's rather than a new arrival.[9]

Anne Boleyn blamed Jane Seymour for her miscarriage, telling the King that she lost their son at fifteen weeks after seeing the new royal mistress sitting on the King's knee.[10] The Queen was increasingly worried about the ascendancy of the Seymours since, on 3 March 1536, Edward Seymour was promoted to the position of a Gentleman of the Privy Chamber, a considerable privilege, whereas she failed to influence the King to invest her brother with the Order of the Garter on 23 April. A political faction hostile to the Boleyns clustered around Jane, who was instructed not to sleep with the King unless he promised her marriage.

Yet in the early days of his infatuation, the King was interested only in bedding Jane, and in late March 1536 he sent her a purse of money with an accompanying letter. When the messenger presented her with these tokens, she fell on her knees and urged him to "pray the King on her part to consider that she was a gentlewoman of good and honourable parents, without reproach, and that she had no greater riches in the world than her honour, which she would not injure for a thousand deaths, and that if he wished to make her some present in money she begged it might be when God enabled her to make some honourable match". This was not exactly what the King wanted to hear, hoping to entice Jane into his bed, but he nevertheless felt that his feelings for her had "wonderfully increased".[11]

It was at that moment that Henry VIII decided that Jane Seymour would replace Anne Boleyn as Queen because he told Jane that he was bent "to show her that he only loved her honourably" and decided he would henceforward visit her only in the company of her relatives. For this purpose, the King ordered Thomas Cromwell to vacate his apartments and give them to Edward and Anne Seymour so that Henry could access them by privy galleries without being perceived by anyone. This is what the King meant when he promised Jane he would pursue her "honourably". During private assignations with Henry VIII, Jane often told the King boldly "how his marriage [to Anne Boleyn] is detested by the people, and none consider it lawful", playing on his desire to do what was right in God's eyes. Anne Seymour played the part of her sister-in-law's chaperone and impatiently waited for what the future held for them.

Like many at the time, the Seymours believed Jane would replace Anne Boleyn as Henry VIII's wife in a scandalous but bloodless coup. Anne, they reasoned, would be divorced and banished from court whether she agreed or not. After all, this happened to Katharine of Aragon, who maintained that she was Henry VIII's legitimate wife until she breathed her last. In late April 1536, John Stokesley, Bishop of London, was approached to give his opinion "as to whether the King could or could not abandon" Anne Boleyn, but he wisely refused to give his verdict unless invited to do so by the King himself.[12] The conspirators often used the words "dismiss" and "divorce" interchangeably when speaking about Anne's ruin. This clearly indicates that they expected Henry VIII to divorce Anne Boleyn and send her away from court in disgrace.

On 2 May 1536, however, Anne Boleyn was arrested at Greenwich Palace and escorted to the Tower of London. Accused of adultery with five men, incest with her brother and plotting to kill the King, the Queen stood little chance of surviving these slanderous allegations. Among the men who were arrested on 5 May 1536 were Sir Henry Norris, the King's Groom of the Stool, Sir Francis Weston, a young courtier whose favourite pastime was to flirt with the Queen's ladies, Sir William Brereton, whose arrest took many by surprise, Mark Smeaton, the musician infatuated with the Queen, and George Boleyn, the Queen's brother.

More arrests followed three days later. On 8 May 1536, one courtier reported that "Mr Page and Mr Wyatt are in the Tower, but it is thought without danger of death".[13] The "Mr Wyatt" was Sir Thomas Wyatt, celebrated Tudor poet and diplomat, whose name had often been linked to Anne Boleyn's. "Mr Page" was Anne Seymour's stepfather. Just why he found himself in the Tower among the men accused as the Queen's paramours is unclear and somewhat surprising considering that he was a member of the extended Seymour family. The rumour mill was grinding ever more furiously, and on 13 May a report circulated at court that "this day, some say, young Weston shall escape, and some that none shall die but the Queen and her brother; others, that Wyatt and Mr Page are as like to suffer as the others."[14]

This scandal in her family did not have an impact on Anne Seymour's career at court, as she was close with the woman who was about to become the next Queen of England.

NOTES

[1] See Appendix 1: When was Anne Seymour born?
[2] *Letters and Papers, Henry VIII,* Volume 4, n. 5016.
[3] Edward Hall, *Hall's Chronicle,* p. 759.
[4] *Letters and Papers, Henry VIII,* Volume 4, n. 5581.
[5] George Cavendish, *The Life of Cardinal Wolsey*, p. 316.
[6] *Letters and Papers, Henry VIII,* Volume 4, n. 6076, 6114.
[7] "Lady Stanhope" appears in the *List of New Year's Gifts Given by and to the King in 1534*, TNA E 101/421/13.

---

[8] Seth Lerer, *Courtly Letters in the Age of Henry VIII: Literary Culture and the Arts of Deceit*, p. 108.

[9] TNA E 101/421/13: *List of New Year's Gifts Given by and to the King in 1534.*

[10] Henry Clifford, *The Life of Jane Dormer, Duchess of Feria*, p. 79.

[11] *Letters and Papers, Henry VIII,* Volume 10, n. 601.

[12] *Calendar of State Papers, Spain,* Volume 5 Part 2, n. 47.

[13] *Letters and Papers, Henry VIII,* Volume 10, n. 855.

[14] Ibid., n. 865.

CHAPTER 2:
THE QUEEN'S SISTER-IN-LAW

In the aftermath of Anne Boleyn's arrest, Jane Seymour was removed from court to Chelsea Manor, where she was "splendidly entertained and served by cooks and officers of the royal household". Queen Anne's royal establishment was disbanded on 13 May 1536, but most of her ladies-in-waiting and officers stayed at court, awaiting further instructions from the King. Anne Seymour was probably one of Jane's female relatives mentioned in the report of the imperial ambassador, Eustace Chapuys, who wrote that she dined with Jane on the morning of Anne Boleyn's trial and later informed Chapuys that the King promised Jane to send her word about his wife's condemnation at three o'clock in the afternoon.[1] At this stage, the Seymours clearly expected the result of Anne Boleyn's trial to be a foregone conclusion, and, indeed, on 15 May 1536 the King sent a messenger to Chelsea informing Jane that the Queen of England had been found guilty of the lurid charges laid against her and condemned to die.

Queen Anne was not the only victim of the coup against her. On 17 May 1536, five innocent men, including the Queen's brother, were executed as her paramours. Anne Seymour's stepfather was fortunate enough to escape with his life, but he was permanently banished from court. On 18 July 1536, he wrote to Lady Honor Lisle from London that he had "not greatly essayed to be a daily courtier again", adding: "And the King being so much my good lord as to give me liberty, I am more meet for the country than the Court."[2]

Anne Boleyn was beheaded with a sword in front of a crowd of one thousand spectators within the confines of the Tower of London on 19 May 1536. The next day Henry VIII arrived at Chelsea Manor and became betrothed to Jane, feasting with her and her family. The couple were married privately at Whitehall Palace ten days later. On 4 June, Jane was proclaimed Queen at Greenwich Palace and was served by a "great train of ladies", many of whom had previously been her colleagues.[3]

Courtiers praised the new Queen, but the public was slowly starting to realize that Henry VIII had been planning his third wedding long before Anne Boleyn was even put on trial, and a certain derogatory ballad started circulating in London at that time. Queen Anne was never popular while alive, but her sudden and shocking execution made the King's subjects suspicious. "There was much muttering of Queen Anne's death", recorded George Constantine, servant of the late Henry Norris, who was beheaded on 17 May. Even the imperial ambassador Eustace Chapuys, who had always detested Anne, was deeply shocked, writing: "The executioner's sword and her own death were virtually to separate and divorce man and wife."[4]

The months following Anne Boleyn's execution were filled with never-ending celebrations and festivities honouring the new Queen and her family. On 6 June 1536, Jane's brother Edward was created Viscount Beauchamp for service "done and to be done; as also of his circumspection, valour and loyalty", and in July he received the office of keeper, governor, and captain of the island of Jersey.[5] Anne Seymour was now a viscountess and was referred to in letters and documents as Lady Beauchamp. She was a visible presence at court, accompanying Queen Jane as her closest and most trusted lady-in-waiting. The Queen had two sisters, Dorothy and Elizabeth, but neither of them served at court, and it appears that they were not very close. As the wife of Jane's beloved brother, Anne naturally took on the role of the Queen's friend and confidante.

Other courtiers quickly recognized Anne's prominence. Lady Honor Lisle, wife of Arthur Plantagenet, Viscount Lisle, was eager to install one of her daughters as maids of honour to Queen Jane. Placing one's child in the royal service required cultivating the good graces of influential ladies-in-waiting, and Lady Lisle, who resided in Calais as wife of the Lord Deputy, sent various letters and gifts to the women she believed would be willing to help her. One of them was Eleanor Manners, Countess of Rutland, who was "in hand with my Lady Beauchamp and other of her friends", trying to help.[6] Queen Jane was not at all eager to take Lady Lisle's daughters into her service, ostensibly because there were no vacancies left.

Yet the real reason behind the Queen's unwillingness was that she saw how Lady Lisle had cultivated the good graces of her fallen predecessor and wanted to keep Lady Lisle on tenterhooks. When the Queen finally appointed the younger and prettier daughter, Anne Basset, she made sure that the girl exchanged her flattering French clothes for heavier and less becoming English styles. Sir John Husee, Lady Lisle's agent, cautioned his employer that she should "not forget to send thanks as well to my Lady Beauchamp as to my Lady of Sussex and my Lady Rutland, for divers causes".[7]

As members of the royal family, Anne and Edward Seymour were entitled to lodgings at court, but they decided to buy a new home for their growing family. In mid-February 1537, the couple acquired Chester Place, their new residence on the London Strand. Anne established her birthing chamber there, and refurbishments to the chapel, where the child was to be christened, were still being carried out when she gave birth to her daughter Jane, named after the Queen. The baby was christened on 22 February 1537.[8] Queen Jane and Lady Mary, the King's elder daughter, stood as godmothers; Thomas Cromwell, Henry VIII's chief minister, was the child's godfather.

Lady Mary had been reinstated to the King's good graces in July 1536 after she submitted herself to his will, accepting that the marriage between her parents was null and void and she herself was a bastard. Since 1533, Mary had opposed her father and refused to accept that Anne Boleyn's daughter, Elizabeth, had supplanted her in the line of succession. After Elizabeth's birth, Mary was stripped of her title of princess and was referred to as Lady Mary, the King's illegitimate daughter. She never accepted that change and persistently called herself the King's heiress and a royal princess. Mary blamed Anne Boleyn for her parents' divorce and her estrangement from her father, but when Anne died she discovered it was the King who still insisted that she was his illegitimate daughter.

From the beginning of her relationship with Henry VIII, Jane Seymour made it clear that she wanted the King to reconcile with his elder daughter and welcome her to court. The King agreed only after pressuring Mary to accept his terms. With the threat of arrest looming large over her, Mary accepted—at least outwardly—that she was the product of an illegitimate marriage. She never believed that, but it was the only way for her to return to court and resume a life appropriate to a lady of her rank and station.

Lady Mary never forgot Queen Jane's efforts on her behalf and established a warm relationship with her. She also became close with Anne Seymour, whom she remembered from her time as Katharine of Aragon's maid of honour. Lady Mary and Anne Seymour would become lifelong friends despite their strong religious differences. In February 1537, Lady Mary paid twenty shillings to Anne's nurse, and in March, after Anne went through the customary ceremony of churching following childbirth, Lady Mary visited her at Chester Place.[9]

At the time of the christening of Anne Seymour's daughter, Queen Jane suspected she was pregnant. In July

1536, just as the new Act of Succession passed through Parliament, allowing the King to designate his own successor, Henry VIII's much beloved bastard son Henry FitzRoy died at the age of seventeen. Many believed that the King wanted FitzRoy to become his heir, but the boy's death destroyed those plans. For the first time in his reign, Henry VIII had no heirs since all of his acknowledged children, including Ladies Mary and Elizabeth, were illegitimate. By autumn of 1536, the King was depressed and started wondering if his wife would be able to give him a son. Henry began to make much of Lady Mary, who was now "the first after the Queen".[10] The King was heard saying that "since his Queen would not give him a son", he wanted to marry his elder daughter to Dom Louis of Portugal so that Mary could give birth to a male heir who would become Henry VIII's successor.[11] Jane Seymour must have been horrified to hear that the King doubted her fertility so openly, knowing that the lack of a male heir had contributed to her predecessor's downfall.

The imperial ambassador described Jane as "no great beauty". She was of middle height and "so fair that one would call her rather pale than otherwise".[12] Despite his initial fascination with her, Henry VIII's eye started to wander early in their marriage. Chapuys gleefully reported how, only eight days after Jane was proclaimed Queen, Henry took notice of two court beauties and "said and showed himself somewhat sorry that he had not seen them before he was married". Beauty aside, Henry was wary of making Jane his anointed Queen, and rumours circulated at court that he postponed her coronation, originally scheduled for the summer of 1536, "to see if she shall be with child".[13] Jane could do little to halt such rumours, but she made certain decisions showing that she was a little more than just a "doormat".[14] Hiding behind a humble motto, "Bound to Obey and Serve", the Queen was as ambitious and jealous as her executed predecessor. Inclined to be "proud and haughty", Jane dismissed the King's former mistress from her service and banned her ladies-in-waiting from wearing seductive French gowns, though she herself owned several French hoods and took full advantage of her royal status, ordering luxurious gowns made of cloth of gold, velvet, damask and other materials.[15] She was in a position to reward her favourites as evidenced by a catalogue of jewels distributed among her ladies. Anne Seymour, catalogued as "Lady Beawham", received various trinkets such as beads for necklaces, girdles to wear around her waist and richly decorated borders for trimming her gowns.[16]

By 23 May 1537, Queen Jane was said to have been "great with child" and started displaying her rounding belly by adding extra panels to her gowns and leaving them unlaced in front.[17] From the very beginning of her pregnancy, Jane was scrutinised by courtiers and the King himself, who ordered the *Te Deum* to be sung and free wine distributed to his subjects when the Queen's baby moved for the first time on 27 May. The pressure to deliver a male heir was unimaginable, and the Queen was well aware that the well-being of her entire family was bound up with the sex of her unborn child.

Queen Jane withdrew from public life in anticipation of her child's birth on 16 September 1537 and delivered a long-awaited son at two o'clock in the morning on 12 October. Her labour dragged on for two long days and three nights until the boy was safely delivered. Later in the prince's life it was remarked that he had a "somewhat projecting shoulder blade", perhaps the result of a prolonged labour, although some said that "the depression in the right shoulder is hereditary in the house of Seymour" and that Anne's husband also had one shoulder lower than the other.[18]

Nicholas Sander, writing in 1585, claimed that "the travail of the Queen being very difficult, the King was asked which of the two lives was to be spared; he answered, the boy's, because he could easily provide himself with other wives."[19] According to this hostile account, Henry VIII was willing to sacrifice the life of Jane to save his child, but there is nothing in contemporary records to support Sander's assertion. Although Jane Seymour's delivery was long and painful, she was strong enough to sign the letters announcing her son's birth. It was a triumphant occasion for the Queen, who succeeded where her two predecessors had failed. Her son was named Edward because he was born on the eve of the feast of the translation of Edward the Confessor.

The christening was a lavish ceremony held in the royal chapel at Hampton Court. A large octagonal platform was raised in the centre of the chapel so that everyone could see the King of England's heir being anointed by the Archbishop of Canterbury. Prince Edward was carried under the canopy of estate by Gertrude Courtenay, Marchioness of Exeter, who was supported on either side by her husband and the Duke of Suffolk. Edward Seymour carried Anne Boleyn's daughter, Elizabeth, who held a richly bejewelled chrisom in her tiny hands. Edward's younger brother Thomas was one of the four knights who bore the canopy of estate above his nephew's head. Behind the canopy walked Lady Mary, the King's daughter, who was her half brother's godmother. After the ceremony, Edward was carried to his parents, who traditionally did not take part in the christening, but awaited him in the antechamber, where the prince received the "blessing of Almighty God, our Lady, and St George, and his father and mother".[20]

Anne and Edward were immediately rewarded as the closest and most trusted relatives of the triumphant Queen. On 18 October 1537, six days after their royal nephew was born, Henry VIII conferred the earldom of Hertford on Edward.[21] Their joy was short-lived, however. In the aftermath of her son's christening, Queen Jane seemed strong and healthy enough to be participating in the post-baptismal ceremony, and plans were made for her imminent churching. But that same evening the Queen began feeling unwell and took to her bed. Day by day, she grew increasingly weak until, on 24 October 1537, she had "a natural lax", loosening of the bowels, after which it looked like she was on the road to full recovery.[22] But Jane's condition worsened that night, and in the morning her confessor came to administer the extreme unction. She was dead before midnight.

Thomas Cromwell, whose son Gregory married the Queen's widowed sister Elizabeth on 3 August 1537, blamed Jane's death on the neglect of her ladies-in-waiting "who suffered her to take cold and eat such things as her fantasy in sickness called for".[23] Yet it was clear to many that the Queen died from postnatal complications. Anne Seymour's initial reaction to her sister-in-law's tragic death is unrecorded, but considering that she was in the early stages of her third pregnancy at the time of Jane's death, she must have been deeply shocked and in fear for her own life during her upcoming delivery.[24]

Ladies who participated in the funeral obsequies that stretched over several days wore "their mourning habits and white kerchiefs hanging over their heads and shoulders" and knelt around the hearse on which the Queen's lifeless body lay in state.[25] During the interment ceremony on 12 November 1537, Lady Mary played the part of chief mourner, but at some point she was replaced by her cousin Frances Grey, Marchioness of Dorset, since she became too distraught to attend. Anne Seymour's name was not recorded among the many ladies of the late Queen's household who rode in chariots following Jane's coffin.

Perhaps, like the Lady Mary, Anne was too heartbroken to attend the funeral of her royal relative, or her pregnancy caused her discomfort and prevented her from attending. Henry VIII mourned the loss of his wife, withdrawing from public life for "a great while".[26] In November 1537, he visited Anne and Edward Seymour at Chester Place, now renamed Beauchamp Place. Also in November, Anne sent baby Jane, accompanied by her nurse, to visit the Lady Mary, perhaps to help the King's daughter through the process of mourning.[27] Although during the period from October 1537 to January 1540 there was no queen to serve, Anne and other ladies at court served the King's daughter, Lady Mary.[28]

On 12 March 1538, Anne gave birth to her third child but first son, named Henry after the King. Henry VIII generously provided luxurious items for the boy's christening, including a rich arras for the chapel at Beauchamp Place and an ornamental cup used during the ceremony.[29] Another son, named Edward after his father, was born on 22 May 1539.[30] It was this boy who would become his father's heir, as their firstborn son, Henry, would die during his childhood.

Although Queen Jane's death slowed their respective careers at court, Anne and Edward Seymour were still highly regarded by the King. In November 1538, Henry VIII invited a small group of his favourites to London, including Anne and Edward. Lady Lisle, who was a member of this prestigious group, wrote excitedly to her husband that they were "highly feasted at supper and after banqueted, and this day dined; and after dinner his Grace showed us all the commodities of this palace [Hampton Court], so that it was night ere we came from thence".[31] Lady Lisle established a close link with the Seymours despite the fact that earlier relations between the Viscount Lisle and Edward Seymour were frosty. Lady Lisle believed that since the Seymours were highly regarded by the King and related to the heir to the throne, their good graces were worth cultivating. She decided to ask Anne and Edward if her daughter Katherine could join their household. The practice of sending gently born children into the service of their family's social equals was well established throughout the Tudor period. Children growing up in such households served their masters but were not servants per se, always treated with the respect of their birthright and counted as part of the family. Girls were taught the art of writing letters, attending the lady's toilette, sewing, embroidering and cooking, as well as managing the estates and supervising servants. Edward Seymour replied favourably to Lady Lisle's request, informing her that he had discussed the matter with Anne, who gladly agreed. He assured Lady Lisle that Katherine Basset would be "as welcome both to me and my wife as any of our own daughters".[32] Yet Katherine Basset, who served in the household of the Countess of Rutland at the time, was loath to leave her mistress and join the Seymours in London. Writing in the twentieth century, a descendant of the Seymour family wrote that Katherine Basset refused to be transferred because "she was certain that Anne Seymour would treat her as a servant", but there is no confirmation of those words in the primary sources. [33]

In August 1539, Henry VIII visited Wolf Hall, the Seymour ancestral seat. The last royal visit had occurred during the King's progress in the summer of 1535. Another royal visit required certain reparations of the manor. Edward Seymour's household accounts show that he paid for necessary renovations to the barn near Wolf Hall, where he and his wife removed while the King and his household occupied the main residence:

"Paid by the hands of Thomas Hethe to certain painters, joiners, carpenters, masons, and others, for their wages in preparing and trimming the Barn at Wolf Hall wherein my Lord lay and kept his house during the King's abode there, and also for the ridding, cleansing and garnishing of the Manor of Wolf Hall wherein the King lay, and also to Penham Lodge where my Lord's mother and children lay."[34]

The King and his large household arrived at Wolf Hall on Saturday, 9 August 1539, and remained until Tuesday. The presence of some four hundred people was recorded on Sunday; they feasted on oxen, mutton, veal, cygnets, capons, pullets, chickens, quails, mews, egrets, shields of brawn, swans, cranes, storks, pheasants, partridges, peachicks, snipe and larks. Fortunately, the King covered much of the costs.

Henry VIII did not stay a widower for long. On 6 January 1540, he married twenty-four-year-old Anne of Cleves. Anne Seymour resumed her career as lady-in-waiting and joined the new Queen's Privy Chamber, but this German bride failed to inspire lust in the King, who conceived an apparent distaste for her physique. Their wedding night was a disaster. The King claimed that his new Queen failed to arouse him sexually because he judged her to be "no maid". Henry scrutinized every inch of his new wife's body, relaying intimate details of her anatomy to the members of his Privy Chamber afterwards. "The looseness of her breasts and other tokens" convinced the King that Anne of Cleves was not a virgin.[35]

Just as this drama was unfolding behind the closed doors of the royal bedchamber, another, no less public, played out in the Seymour family. In April 1540, Edward Seymour's eldest son from his first marriage to Catherine Fillol, John, was debarred from succeeding his father. The second son of this marriage, Edward, would inherit his father's titles, lands and manors only if Edward Seymour had no male heirs with Anne or with any subsequent wife.[36] It was suggested in the seventeenth century that Edward disinherited Catherine Fillol's sons because he believed she had committed adultery and the boys were not his. Some writers suggested that the man with whom Fillol had an affair was her own father-in-law, Sir John Seymour, yet there is no hint of this in the primary sources; quite the contrary. When Queen Jane refused to become Henry VIII's mistress, she argued that she was "the daughter of good and honourable parents without blame or reproach of any kind".[37] Would Jane really utter such a remark if her father was widely known to have committed incest[38] with Catherine Fillol? It is doubtful.

It seems that Sir John had a good reputation among his contemporaries because when Henry VIII married Jane Seymour on 30 May 1536, chronicler Edward Hall recorded that Jane was the "daughter of the right worshipful Sir John Seymour, knight".[39] It is highly likely that the story about Sir John Seymour's alleged incest with Catherine Fillol stems from the fact that Catherine named her firstborn son John, and Sir John Seymour was known to have had an illegitimate son also named, confusingly, John. The suggestion of incest probably stems from a marginal note in *Vincent's Baronage* in the College of Arms, *"repudiata quia pater ejus post nuptias eam cognovit"*, which means "because she was known [in carnal sense] by his father after the nuptials".[40]

Edward Seymour must have had grave reasons to doubt the paternity of his sons by Catherine. Catherine was placed in a nunnery, another hint that she may have conducted an extramarital affair. Her father's last will composed in 1527 also hints at a scandal involving Catherine. Sir William Fillol stipulated that his daughter should receive an annuity of £40 "as long as she shall live virtuously and abide in some house of religion of women." He also stipulated that "for many diverse causes and considerations" neither Catherine "nor her heirs of her body, nor Sir Edward Seymour her husband in any wise" were to inherit "any part or parcel" of his estates.[41]

Anne Seymour was certainly glad that her sons, who were undoubtedly Edward's, had precedence over the children of dubious paternity. Yet some twelve years later John Seymour would be reinstated to Edward's estates by an act of Parliament, according to which he had been debarred from succeeding Edward through "corrupt and sinister labour by the power of his second wife over him".[42] It is doubtful that Anne turned Edward against his sons. Any man who doubted his children's paternity would act in similar fashion, bestowing the succession of his titles and lands on children who were his without any shadow of doubt.

NOTES

[1] *Calendar of State Papers, Spain,* Volume 5 Part 2, n. 55.
[2] Muriel St Clare Byrne, *The Lisle Letters,* Volume 3, p. 460.
[3] Charles Wriothesley, *A Chronicle of England During the Reigns of the Tudors,* Volume 1, p. 44.
[4] *Calendar of State Papers, Spain,* Volume 5 Part 2, n. 72.
[5] Helen St Maur, *Annals of the Seymours,* p. 377.
[6] Muriel St Clare Byrne, *The Lisle Letters,* Volume 4, p. 139.
[7] Ibid., p. 163.
[8] Ibid., p. 122. See also *Appendix 2: Children of Anne and Edward Seymour.*
[9] Frederic Madden, *Privy Purse Expenses of the Princess Mary,* pp. 16, 19.
[10] *Letters and Papers, Henry VIII,* Volume 11, n. 860.
[11] *Calendar of State Papers, Spain,* Volume 5 Part 2, n. 116.

---

12 *Letters and Papers, Henry VIII*, Volume 10, n. 901.
13 Ibid., Volume 11, n. 8.
14 Leslie Carroll, *Notorious Royal Marriages*, p. 121.
15 *Letters and Papers, Henry VIII,* Volume 10, n. 901.
16 Ibid., Volume 12 Part 2, n. 973.
17 Muriel St Clare Byrne, *The Lisle Letters*, Volume 4, p. 144.
18 Henry Morley, *Lives of Physicians*, Volume 2, p. 135. *Calendar of State Papers, Spain,* Volume 11, 1553, 17 February 1553.
19 Nicholas Sander, *The Rise and Growth of the Anglican Schism*, p. 138.
20 John Gough Nichols, *Literary Remains of King Edward the Sixth*, Volume 1, p. cclvi.
21 *Letters and Papers, Henry VIII,* Volume 12 Part 2, n. 939.
22 Peter Heylyn, *Ecclesia Restaurata*, Volume 1, p. 15.
23 *Letters and Papers, Henry VIII,* Volume 12 Part 2, n. 1004.
24 In April 1538, Lady Mary "paid to my Lady Kingston for money by her laid out at the christening of my Lady of Sussex's child and my Lady of Hertford's child". Frederic Madden, *Privy Purse Expenses of the Princess Mary*, p. 65.
25 *Letters and Papers, Henry VIII,* Volume 12 Part 2, n. 1060.
26 Edward Hall, *Hall's Chronicle*, p. 825.
27 Frederic Madden, *Privy Purse Expenses of the Princess Mary*, pp. 46.
28 *Letters and Papers, Henry VIII,* Volume 13 Part 2, 1280, f. 55.
29 Sarah Morris, Natalie Grueninger, *In the Footsteps of the Six Wives of Henry VIII*, p. 191. *Letters and Papers, Henry VIII,* Volume 13 Part 2, n. 1280 (f. 17).
30 Muriel St Clare Byrne, *The Lisle Letters*, Volume 5, pp. 493, 508.
31 Ibid., pp. 282, 285.
32 Ibid., p. 508.
33 William Seymour, *Ordeal By Ambition*, p. 125.
34 Rev. John Edward Jackson, *Wulfhall and the Seymours*, p. 7.
35 H.A. Kelly, *The Matrimonial Trials of Henry VIII*, p. 270.
36 *Letters and Papers, Henry VIII,* Volume 15, n. 498, C. 78 [o. n. 74].
37 *Calendar of State Papers, Spain*, Volume 5 Part 2, n. 43.
38 Catherine was Sir John's daughter-in-law and a sexual relationship between them would be termed as incest.
39 Edward Hall, *Hall's Chronicle*, p. 819.
40 Carole Levin, Anna Riehl Bertolet, *A Biographical Encyclopaedia of Early Modern Englishwomen*, p. 174.
41 Wilbur Kitchener Jordan, *Edward VI: The Young King: The Protectorship of the Duke of Somerset*, p. 46.
42 Wilbur Kitchener Jordan, *Edward VI: Treshold of Power*, p. 337.

CHAPTER 3: BRUSH WITH TREASON

Within six months of their January wedding, Anne of Cleves's marriage to Henry VIII was annulled and the King hastily tied the knot with the teenaged Katherine Howard, niece of Thomas Howard, Duke of Norfolk. On the day of his fifth wedding, the King sent Thomas Cromwell, his chief minister and the architect of the Cleves match, to the scaffold. Anne Seymour's sister-in-law, Elizabeth, found herself in a difficult situation. Happily married to Cromwell's son, Gregory, Elizabeth now feared that her father-in-law's "most grievous offences" would influence the lives of her children.[1] Incarcerated in the Tower, Cromwell begged the King "to be good and gracious lord to my poor son, the good and virtuous lady his wife, and their poor children".[2] Henry VIII obliged and elevated Gregory Cromwell to the status of Baron Cromwell. The Cromwell and Seymour families were unaffected by Thomas Cromwell's execution.

Anne Seymour joined Katherine Howard's household as an experienced lady-in-waiting, but she did not establish a close relationship with her. When salacious allegations of sexual misconduct prior to her royal marriage were brought against the Howard Queen by John Lascelles in the autumn of 1541, Anne's husband was among the first who interrogated him and later advised the Archbishop of Canterbury to reveal the Queen's crimes to Henry VIII.

Katherine Howard was beheaded on 13 February 1542, together with her lady-in-waiting Jane Boleyn, sister-in-law of the executed Queen Anne. Katherine was accused of committing adultery with Thomas Culpeper, member of the King's Privy Chamber, and leading an immoral life in the household of her step-grandmother, Agnes Howard, Dowager Duchess of Norfolk, prior to her marriage to Henry VIII. The King, who sincerely loved his fifth wife, was plunged into a deep depression, and many believed he would never remarry, being wary of "taking young wives".[3] Yet on 12 July 1543, Henry VIII married for the sixth and last time "in presence of the noble and gentle persons", including Edward and Anne Seymour.[4] The King's new wife was Katherine Parr, a twice-widowed lady two years younger than Anne. Anne joined the Queen's household as one of the "great ladies", and the two women got along together exceptionally well. Both were interested in religious reform and believed that women should have free access to learning. By the time Katherine Parr became

Queen, Anne Seymour had served at court for more than a decade and was the mother of a still-growing brood of offspring. Anne and her husband provided equal educational opportunities for all of their children and were praised by the intellectual Thomas Becon for employing "all their endeavours to train them up, even from their very cradles, in good letters and in the knowledge of God's most blessed will".[5]

The most important relationship in Anne's life was that with her husband. They were a harmonious, loving couple, as attested by numerous letters they exchanged as well as the public perception of Anne as Edward's confidante. In 1542, Thomas Wriothesley informed Edward, who was serving on a military campaign in Scotland, that Anne "will not be merry until she hears from you".[6] In June 1544, while pregnant with another child, Anne used her influence with the Queen and reminded her of her promise to recall Edward from the north, where he served as Warden of the Scottish Marches. Katherine Parr replied:

"Madam, my lord your husband's coming hither is not altered, for he shall come home before the King's majesty takes his journey over the seas, as it pleased His Majesty to declare to me of late. You may be right assured I would not have forgotten my promise to you in a matter of less effect than this, and so I pray you most heartily to think. And thus with my very hearty commendations to you I end, wishing you so well to fare as I would myself.

Your assured friend,

Katherine the Queen, K.P."[7]

Anne returned to court after the christening of her child that took place in August 1544. Katherine Parr may have been the child's godmother since she paid her servant Kirton for rowing her "to the Earl of Hertford's house" on that occasion.[8]

The Queen's household soon became a centre of learned religious discussions. John Foxe, the author of *Book of Martyrs*, wrote that Katherine Parr was "much given to the reading and study of the Holy Scriptures" and that every day in the afternoon she held regular meetings with her chaplains, ladies-in-waiting and "others that were disposed to hear". The Queen would serve refreshments in her Privy Chamber and listen to hour-long sermons that were followed by enlivened discussions about "such abuses as in the church then were rife".[9]

The court was divided into two factions: Catholic and Protestant. The Catholics were led by Stephen Gardiner, Bishop of Winchester, who was eager to purge the King's circle of "heretics", people who dared to question the Church doctrine and read the Bible for themselves. The evangelicals within the Privy Council assumed an increasingly important role on the political and religious front, several of them being Henry VIII's closest friends and advisers. "The King favours these stirrers of heresy, the Earl of Hertford [Edward Seymour] and Lord Admiral [John Dudley, Viscount Lisle]", wrote the indignant imperial ambassador Chapuys, adding that he suspected this was because "the Queen, instigated by the Duchess of Suffolk [Katherine Brandon], Countess of Hertford and the Admiral's wife [Jane Dudley], shows herself infected".[10]

Anne Seymour was named among the "stirrers of heresy" who influenced Katherine Parr's religious views. When Stephen Gardiner decided to strike at the Queen, accusing her of heresy, her ladies-in-waiting became his targets as well. Katherine Parr often initiated heated debates about religion and thrived when the King gave ear to her opinions. What she did not know was that Henry VIII was growing irritated by her commanding tone and lack of deference to his judgment. Gardiner used this to his own advantage and received the King's permission to investigate the Queen's circle.

In the summer of 1546, a young gentlewoman, Anne Askew, was arrested and questioned about her seditious religious views. She was very vocal in expressing them, and it was believed that she had friends among Katherine Parr's ladies-in-waiting. Gardiner hoped that Askew would break under vigorous interrogation and implicate the Queen and her ladies. Brutally tortured by Thomas Wriothesley and Richard Rich, Askew later testified that "they did put me on the rack because I confessed no ladies or gentlemen to be of my opinion". While tortured, Anne Askew was asked about her relationship with the Queen's ladies such as "my Lady of Suffolk, my Lady of Sussex, my Lady of Hertford, my Lady Denny and my Lady Fitzwilliam". It was clear the interrogators wanted to strike at these women and their husbands.

The closest Askew came to implicating Anne Seymour was when she confessed that "there was a man in a blue coat who delivered me ten shillings, and said that my Lady of Hertford sent it".[11] Financial support of a woman who held views that the government perceived as seditious was certainly dangerous, but it proves that Anne Seymour's religious beliefs were genuine. Yet this was not enough to accuse Katherine Parr, Anne Seymour or any other ladies of the Queen's Privy Chamber of heresy. Anne Askew, maimed and in pain after the inhumane torture sessions that sent shockwaves across the country, was carried to her execution in a chair. She was burned at the stake on 16 July 1546.

The Seymours emerged triumphant from this factional power struggle. Five months after Anne Askew's execution, the new imperial ambassador, Francis van der Delft, observed that the persecutions stopped when Edward Seymour resumed regular residency at court and that "the meetings of the Council are mostly held in the Earl of Hertford's house".[12] The King was surrounded by reformers, men whom he trusted and relied on. Edward Seymour was their leader, and many sought his favors when it became apparent that the King's health was rapidly deteriorating. As he limped through his declining years, Henry VIII gained so much weight that supporting his massive bulk on richly carved walking sticks became impossible, and he had to be moved about in a sedan chair carried by four attendants. On 28 January 1547, Henry VIII—obese, immobile and with ulcers on his legs oozing malodorous puss—breathed his last at Whitehall Palace, surrounded by his trusted advisors. His death ushered a new dawn into Tudor England. With the nine-year-old boy King on the throne, Edward Seymour would become a king in all but name, and Anne would be there beside him to fulfill her duties as the primary hostess at court.

NOTES

[1] M.A. Everett Wood, *Letters of Royal and Illustrious Ladies of Great Britain*, Volume 3, p. 159.
[2] *Letters and Papers, Henry VIII,* Volume 15, n. 824.
[3] *Chronicle of King Henry VIII (The Spanish Chronicle)*, p. 107.
[4] *Letters and Papers, Henry VIII,* Volume 18 Part 1, n. 873.
[5] Thomas Becon, *The Early Works of Thomas Becon*, p. 396.
[6] *Letters and Papers, Henry VIII,* Volume 17, n. 1067.
[7] Janel Mueller, *Katherine Parr: Complete Works and Correspondence*, p. 79.
[8] *Letters and Papers, Henry VIII,* Volume 19 Part 2, n. 688.
[9] John Foxe, *The Actes and Monuments of John Foxe*, Volume 5, p. 554.
[10] *Letters and Papers, Henry VIII,* Volume 21 Part 2, n. 756.
[11] Ibid., Volume 21 Part 1, n. 1181.
[12] *Calendar of State Papers, Relating to England and Spain,* Volume 6, p. 533-534.

CHAPTER 4:
SCANDALS AND RIVALRIES

Henry VIII's death and his son's accession heralded a new dawn for Anne Seymour and the women at court. The nine-year-old Prince Edward, now King Edward VI, was too young to rule in his own right, and Henry VIII had made necessary provisions for his son's guidance and government in the last weeks of his life. He designated that sixteen executors of his last will would constitute a Council of Regency, with twelve other advisors. The old King made it luminously clear that he wanted decisions to be taken by a majority vote and that there would be no one individual who would have pre-eminence over the others. Yet Henry VIII's last will was thwarted immediately after his death. On 31 January 1547, Anne Seymour's ambitious husband, Edward, Earl of Hertford, was sworn in as Lord Protector and declared as a "special man . . . preferred in name and place before others". Edward was singled out because he was the new King's uncle as well as because of the "great experience which he hath in all the affairs of this realm".[1] On 7 February 1547, Edward Seymour was created Duke of Somerset.[2] The dukedom of Somerset linked Edward and

Anne directly to the royalty: the title was borne by Henry VII's Beaufort ancestors and later conferred on this King's youngest son, Edmund, who died in his early childhood. Henry VIII revived this title by conferring the double dukedoms of Richmond and Somerset onto his illegitimate son Henry FitzRoy, who died in 1536. "The Protector governs absolutely", wrote the imperial ambassador Van der Delft, adding that he always did so "on the advice of Secretary Paget".[3]

What kind of a man was Edward Seymour? A portrait dating to his time as Earl of Hertford depicts a stern-looking man with deep-set hazel eyes and a long brown beard, proudly displaying his chain of the Order of the Garter. As to his character, early in his nephew's reign he was described as "a dry, sour, opinionated man", yet it is clear that he was much more than that.[4] An accomplished soldier, talented in statecraft and interested in religious reform, Somerset understood that he owed his position entirely to his blood relation to the King. When, soon after Henry VIII's death, Somerset was approached by his brother Thomas to obtain permission to marry Lady Mary, the King's elder half sister, Edward's reply encapsulated his thoughts on his elevation:

"The Protector was displeased and reproved him, saying that neither of them was born to be King, nor to marry kings' daughters; and though God had given them grace that their sister should have married a King, whence so much honour and benefit had redounded to them, they must thank God and be satisfied; besides which he knew the Lady Mary would never consent."[5]

Yet, as soon became evident, Edward Seymour felt that being related to the King gave him an aura of royalty and set him apart from others at court—and Anne shared his belief. Aware that their new status should be expressed through clothing, shortly after establishing the protectorate Somerset arranged for the transfer of furs from some of Henry VIII's gowns to his own clothes so that he could wear them during Edward VI's coronation. He also made sure that his wife looked the part and took possession of some of the royal jewels belonging to Henry VIII and his six wives—an action many believed was a step too far.[6]

Edward Seymour's new position was met with the approval of his fellow councillors, but Edward VI's stepmother, Katherine Parr, was disappointed. The Dowager Queen had hoped that Henry VIII would appoint her as regent for the young King, and she believed Edward and his adherents in the Privy Council had tampered with the late King's last will. Katherine had successfully conducted her role as Regent of England during Henry VIII's absence on a war campaign in France in 1544 and expected this position to be conferred on her again. Yet Henry VIII's last will made it clear that he did not envisage Katherine as regent during Edward VI's minority, but neither had it designated one man as Lord Protector. Effectively robbed of her chance to exert political influence in the newly formed regime, Katherine Parr now decided to concentrate on her private life, withdrawing from permanent residence at the King's court to one of her dower estates, Chelsea Manor. The Dowager Queen's seemingly private decision to remarry would set her on a path toward an epic clash with Anne Seymour and her husband.

Before she married Henry VIII, Katherine had fallen in love with Edward Seymour's rakish younger brother Thomas. Handsome, athletic and ambitious, Thomas reciprocated her feelings and proposed marriage within days of Henry VIII's death. The thirty-five-year-old Dowager Queen was torn between duty and her own desires. After three marriages—her husbands were either mentally incapacitated or past their prime—she still had no offspring, although she yearned to have a child of her own.

As a royal widow, she was expected to wait at least two years before marrying again, but she was not getting any younger, and Thomas urged her "to change the two years into two months". Before she agreed, Katherine emphasized that her decision did not proceed from "any sudden motion or passion" because she was in love with Thomas before the King started courting her.[7] Katherine could not resist Thomas's charm, and the couple soon embarked in a love affair. Their secret marriage probably took place before 17 May 1547 since, in one of his love letters addressed to Katherine, Thomas referred to himself as her husband: "from him whom ye have bound to honour, love, and such in all lawful thing obey". Katherine reciprocated, signing herself as "her that is and shall be your humble, true and loving wife during her life".[8] The couple understood that their wedding was very hasty and could meet with opposition from the influential members of Edward VI's circle since, as Dowager Queen, Katherine was expected not only to mourn her royal husband at least two years, but also obtain the Privy Council's approval for remarriage.

Katherine and Thomas decided to seek the support of Anne and Edward Seymour, who were now the most influential people in England. The Dowager Queen expected her former lady-in-waiting, who was now her sister-in-law, to accept her marriage to Thomas, yet Anne would prove to be the couple's staunchest opponent. When Katherine went to court to see the Lord Protector in the winter of 1547, he deferred his decision about her dower lands, although he had previously promised her a favourable outcome. "This is not the first promise I have received of his coming, and yet unperformed", Katherine wrote resentfully to Thomas. She blamed Anne, whom she believed influenced her husband: "I think my Lady hath taught him that lesson, for it is her custom to promise many comings to her friends, and to perform none. I trust in greater matters she is more circumspect."[9]

When Thomas saw Anne at court in early May 1547, he asked her if she would be willing to meet with Katherine the next day, but Anne had other plans: "My Lady of Somerset told me on Friday night that she would [go] to Sheen at the next day, and at her return on Tuesday, which is tomorrow, she would see your Highness." "I pray you, if you see yourself in good credit with her, to desire her grace to be my good lady", Thomas wrote to Katherine but added that "if I see myself in more favour than you, I shall make the like request for you". Yet by 17 May, Anne had still not spoken to Katherine, as she delayed her trip to Sheen because of a sickness and planned to travel there with her husband. Katherine and Thomas decided to change tactics, and the Dowager Queen suggested Thomas could try to approach his brother directly, but, as is evident from Katherine's letter, Thomas was reluctant: "I gather by your letter . . . you are in some fear how to frame my lord your brother to speak in your favour."[10]

Thomas, like Katherine, resented his brother's role of Lord Protector and was angry that he held no prominent place in the new regime. Upon Edward VI's accession, Thomas was made Baron of Sudeley, a meagre reward considering Edward's newly conferred ducal status, and received the title of Lord Admiral. He also resented the fact that Anne Seymour's stepfather, Sir Richard Page, and her half brother, Sir Michael Stanhope, controlled the access to Edward VI's Privy Chamber and kept the young King largely isolated from the outside world.

Katherine Parr also had reasons to resent the Lord Protector's influence. The Dowager Queen was disenchanted with Edward Seymour when he began granting leases on her dower lands without her approval and refused to restore her jewels. The jewels were an especially delicate subject with Katherine since they included pieces she received from Henry VIII as gifts, such as her golden wedding ring and a crown-headed brooch, and her personal property, such as the jewellery her mother willed to her in 1531. Katherine deposited these valuables in the royal treasury in the Tower for safekeeping after Henry VIII's death, but when she wanted to withdraw them, Edward Seymour refused to give them back, arguing that the jewels were the property of the Crown and not Katherine's private possessions. At this point, the Lord Protector already suspected that Katherine had secretly married his brother and believed that since she was now only Lady Seymour, she had no right to adorn herself with royal jewellery that was reserved for a reigning consort.

At the end of May 1547, Katherine went to see her brother-in-law at court. She broached the subject of her marriage to Thomas but met with cold resistance on Edward's part. She also finally managed to schedule a meeting with Anne Seymour, but the Duchess of Somerset backed her husband instead of her former royal mistress. In a letter to Thomas, Katherine mused: "What cause have they to fear [you] having such a wife?" The relationship between the Dowager Queen and Anne Seymour had already disintegrated at this point, and Katherine called her former servant "that hell".[11] Seeing that neither Edward nor Anne were eager to help, Katherine and Thomas decided to enlist the help of Lady Mary and King Edward VI. To better achieve their goal, Katherine and Thomas decided to keep their private wedding secret until they obtained the blessings of Henry VIII's children.

Lady Mary was stunned when Thomas Seymour revealed that he wanted to marry Katherine Parr. She refused to be "a meddler in this matter, considering whose wife her grace was of late". If, Mary added, Katherine favoured his matrimonial suit, her recommendation would "do you but small pleasure". The wording of Mary's eloquent epistle suggests that she hoped that Katherine would not hurry into a new marriage; "if the remembrance of the King's majesty, my father . . . will not suffer her to grant your suit, I am nothing able to persuade her to forget the loss of him, who is as yet very ripe in mine own remembrance".[12]

If Katherine Parr expected her former stepdaughter to endorse her marriage, she was bitterly disappointed. The two had formed a close relationship while Katherine was Henry VIII's wife, but apparently not as close as Mary shared with Anne Seymour. In April 1547, Mary wrote to the Duchess of Somerset on behalf of two servants who served in Katharine of Aragon's household. Affectionately addressing Anne as "my good Gossip", Lady Mary requested Anne speak with her husband about "mine old suit concerning Richard Wood, who was my mother's servant when you were one of her Grace's maids". The Duchess of Somerset was fond of Lady Mary, as evidenced by Mary's effusive note wherein she thanked "my good Nan . . . for your earnest gentleness towards me in all my suits hitherto, reckoning myself out of doubt of the continuance of the same".[13] It is clear that Anne wanted to cultivate Mary's good graces and that she interceded with her husband on her behalf. Mary's suit was successful, and she later thanked Edward Seymour "for his attention to her requests as to pensions for some of her servants".[14]

In June 1547, Katherine Parr and Thomas Seymour obtained Edward VI's permission to marry, but they still failed to mention that the wedding had already taken place. Later that month the imperial ambassador Van der Delft informed the emperor that "I have been informed from a secret source that a marriage is being arranged between the Dowager Queen and the Lord Admiral, brother of the Protector". Two months later, on 10 July, the ambassador reported that "the Queen was married a few days since to the Lord Admiral", suggesting that the couple went through another, this time public, wedding ceremony. Van der Delft also added that Katherine "still causes herself to be served ceremoniously as Queen, which it appears is the custom here".[15] The fact that Katherine Parr retained a large royal household and insisted on using the title of Dowager Queen enraged Anne Seymour and her husband, who was "much offended" at his brother's marriage.[16] In the absence of a Queen consort at Edward VI's side, the Duchess of Somerset believed that she was the most important woman in the kingdom. After all, she was the King's aunt by marriage, and her husband was Lord Protector. Edward Seymour concurred since he sought means to elevate himself above his fellow councillors; he had a special place in Parliament, adopted a royal "we" when signing letters and occupied the Queen's side of the royal palaces instead of using the lodgings designated unto him during Henry VIII's reign.[17] Even Edward's new coat of arms incorporated the armorial bearings used by his late sister, Queen Jane, and proclaimed Seymour's "unfounded connection to the kings of England".[18] The imperial ambassador, who invited Edward to act as a godfather to his son in May 1547, observed that the Lord Protector was determined "to take the first place on every occasion".[19]

By February 1548, the animosity between the two Seymour couples was palpable. Odet de Selve, the French ambassador, reported that a dispute arose between Edward and Thomas Seymour because of the discord between their wives.[20] A contemporary *Chronicle of King Henry VIII*, written by an anonymous Spaniard in the 1550s and thus commonly known as *The Spanish Chronicle*, identifies the root of this discord as a quarrel over precedence between Anne Seymour and Katherine Parr. According to the chronicler, Anne believed that since her "husband ruled the kingdom she ought to be more considered than the Queen, and claimed to take precedence of her". On one occasion, the chronicler wrote, Anne had even physically shoved Katherine in the royal chapel, thrusting herself forward and taking the Queen's seat. The chronicler put the following words into Katherine Parr's mouth:

"How is this that through my marriage with you the wife of your brother is treating me with contempt and presumes to go before me? I will never allow it, for I am Queen, and shall be called so all my life, and I promise you if she does again what she did yesterday [in the chapel] I will pull her back myself."

When Edward, who allowed himself "to be more ruled by his wife's desires than anything else", approached Thomas, he asked:

"Brother, are you not my younger brother, and am I not Protector, and do you not know that your wife, before she married the King, was of lower rank than my wife? I desire, therefore, since the Queen is your wife that mine should go before her."[21]

The Spanish Chronicle is not the most reliable of sources, but it offers a reflection of contemporary thought. Other, more trustworthy sources confirm that some sort of a power struggle had indeed occurred between Anne Seymour and Katherine Parr. The most reliable one is Thomas Seymour himself, who, after the birth of his daughter, Mary, in September 1548, mused that "it would be strange to some when his daughter came of age, taking her place above the Duchess of Somerset, as a Queen's daughter". Also, one of Thomas's servants admitted that Anne bore Thomas ill will only "for the Queen's cause".[22] It is likely that Anne believed that since Katherine had committed a mésalliance when marrying Thomas, she should lose her royal title. She was not the only one who thought so. When Lady Mary asked Odet de Selve what he thought about Katherine Parr's hasty remarriage, the ambassador condemned the Dowager Queen for having been "content to forget the honour she had enjoyed from the late King".[23] Mary, who still mourned her late father by wearing black and refusing to dine in public, had also quietly condemned her stepmother's actions.

As the wife of Baron Seymour of Sudeley, Katherine Parr's social rank was indeed inferior to Anne Seymour's, but it was not uncommon for widows in England to retain a higher rank after marrying a social inferior. Henry VIII's younger sister, Mary Tudor, for instance, married Charles Brandon, Duke of Suffolk, after her husband, Louis XII of France, died in January 1515. Mary was a crowned Queen of France, and she retained that title, signing her letters as "Mary the French Queen" until her death, although she also occasionally used the title of Duchess of Suffolk. Yet Katherine Parr was not a crowned Queen. Before she married the King, she was only "Latimer's widow". Anne Seymour clearly believed that she was now above Katherine; she could claim a drop of royal blood herself since through her mother she was a descendant of Edward III.[24]

Katherine, eager to maintain her royal status, created a household that rivalled that of any other woman in England. Thomas Seymour was especially keen to emphasize that he had married into the highest echelon of nobility and was eager to uphold his wife's "princely royalty". Katherine soon had a large court with 120 servants, including "the gentlewomen of the Queen's Highness's Privy Chamber . . . and also the maids which waited at large and other women being about her Grace".[25] She had twenty-six ladies-in-waiting, seven maids of honour, with a Mother of the Maids, who supervised them, six gentlewomen of the Privy Chamber and five chamberers.[26]

Nobility still flocked to Katherine's new establishment that was termed "a second court" and rivalled the household of the Duke and Duchess of Somerset.[27] Additionally, the Dowager Queen took Lady Elizabeth, Henry VIII's younger daughter, to her establishment, and Thomas Seymour managed to buy the wardship of Lady Jane Grey, granddaughter of Mary the French Queen. The presence of these two royal ladies at her court added further prestige to Katherine Parr's status.

If Anne Seymour believed that Katherine Parr's withdrawal from Edward VI's court meant she would settle for a quiet rural life, she was mistaken. Early in 1548, another scandal linked to the Dowager Queen's household spurred fresh ripples of salacious gossip at court. This time Katherine decided to help her brother, William Parr, Marquis of Northampton, who wished to remarry. William's arranged marriage to Anne Bourchier had taken place on 9 February 1527, when he was thirteen and she ten. Bourchier, an heiress of the Earl of Essex, was a splendid match, but the couple had little in common. William was horrified when his wife committed adultery in 1541. When she eloped with her lover and gave birth to his illegitimate child, William took legal steps to ensure that his unfaithful wife's children would never be able to inherit his titles.[28] Divorce did not exist in Henry VIII's England, and William's only chance at remarriage was his wife's death. But after the old King's demise, William decided to legalise his long-term relationship with Elisabeth Brooke, daughter of George Brooke, ninth Baron Cobham, and his wife, Anne Braye.

Born on 12 June 1526, Elisabeth Brooke was young, beautiful and vivacious. She was first mentioned at court in 1542 as one of the ladies to whom Henry VIII paid much attention during a banquet he held after his fifth wife's execution. She was then described as "a pretty young creature, with wit enough to do as badly as the others if she were to try".[29] Elisabeth's mother, Anne Brooke, Baroness Cobham, served as a lady-in-waiting to Anne Boleyn and was said to have been one of the "first accusers" who stepped forward with damning accusations of the Queen's adultery in 1536.[30] Elisabeth started her career at court in 1542 and served as a maid of honour to Katherine Parr from 1543 to 1547. Young and impressionable, she easily fell in love with the older William Parr. He was not only learned and wealthy, but also incredibly handsome and the epitome of a perfect courtier, "a man very well-versed in the more delightful sort of studies as music, love-toys, and other courtly dalliances".[31]

Trapped in a loveless marriage, Parr had engaged in an extramarital affair with Dorothy Braye, Elisabeth's aunt. The affair was notorious, and even Queen Katherine Howard teased her lover, Thomas Culpeper, saying that she could "bring you into as good a trade as Braye hath my lord Parr in".[32] By 1545, Parr's relationship with Dorothy was over, and he set his sights on Elisabeth. That autumn she stayed at court while her parents moved to Calais, where her father served as Lord Deputy. On 30 November 1545, John Wilkins, servant of Elisabeth's parents, reported to Baron Cobham that he "was with Mrs Elisabeth at Court on Thursday last, and talked with her but a while" since she was attending Lady Mary on their way to the Duchess of Suffolk's house, where they were taking part in the christening of Sir John Dudley's child. Elisabeth's parents were apparently worried about their daughter's relationship with William Parr, who was, after all, a married man, and ordered Wilkins to talk to Mrs Stonor, who served as Mother of the Maidens and supervised their behaviour. Wilkins dutifully reported to Lord and Lady Cobham that Mrs Stonor assured him that "there was nothing in Mistress Elisabeth's doings that was to be misliked".[33] It soon became apparent that William Parr's relationship with Elisabeth Brooke was not a mere courtly dalliance. Unlike her aunt Dorothy, Elisabeth understood that a damaged reputation was not easily repaired. She may have kept Parr at arm's length, hoping for something more than just a passing flirtation.

In early 1548, the imperial ambassador Van der Delft reported that he had been told in strict confidence that William Parr married Elisabeth Brooke "by means of his sister the Queen and of the Duchess of Suffolk [Katherine Brandon] . . . and that eight or nine days afterwards he was obliged by the command of the Council to put her away and never speak to her again on pain of death, in consequence of his having already a wife living, although he has long been separated from her".[34] The ambassador's informer was correct. On 31 January 1548, Edward Seymour set up a commission to investigate whether the marriage had indeed taken place. The Lord

Protector decided to order Elisabeth Brooke to stay in the household of Katherine Parr, her sister-in-law, until the matter was cleared. She was forbidden to live or communicate with William.

This was not the end of the scandals that originated in the household of Katherine Parr. Lady Elizabeth, the Dowager Queen's stepdaughter, had lived with Katherine and Thomas since the summer of 1547. At some point, Thomas made it his habit to visit Elizabeth's bedchamber before she was out of bed, wishing her "good morrow and ask how she did, or strike her upon the back". If he found her still in bed, Seymour would draw back the bed curtains, bid her "good morrow" and "make as though he would come at her". Seymour often came to Elizabeth's bedchamber dressed only in his nightgown, "bare legged and in his slippers", but he usually found her reading a book. Elizabeth made it her habit to rise early in order to be dressed before Seymour's visitation, although she had once stated she was not a "morning woman". Elizabeth's governess, Kat Ashley, chastised Seymour and told him that "it was an unseemly sight to come so bare legged to a maiden's chamber".[35]

The implication of invading a virgin's private space like that held a dangerous sexual undertone. During the Tudor period, men made a show of their muscular legs by wearing tight, leg-hugging stockings beneath their knee-length tunics. Legs and knees often symbolised the most intimate, hidden parts of one's body. Even marriages were symbolically consummated when the bare leg of a woman was touched by a man's bare foot; it was so common that a famous Tudor proverb said that "there belonged more to a marriage than two pairs of bare legs". Kat Ashley told Katherine Parr about Seymour's behaviour, but the Dowager Queen "made a small matter of it" and volunteered to visit Elizabeth's bedchamber with Seymour—and they did so together, adding more awkwardness to the situation. On one occasion, when the Dowager Queen was walking with Elizabeth in the gardens, Seymour approached Elizabeth and "cut her gown in a hundred pieces" while Katherine held her back.

Details of Thomas Seymour's romps in Elizabeth's chambers soon spread across the country and reached the ears of Anne Seymour, who was shocked at the lack of discipline in Katherine Parr's household. She blamed Elizabeth's wayward governess, Kat Ashley, for allowing Seymour to dally with Henry VIII's daughter and took it upon herself to berate Kat in very strong terms. Anne rebuked Kat for allowing Elizabeth to travel by barge on the Thames late at night and for other "light parts". The Duchess of Somerset told Kat that "she was not worthy to have the governance of a King's daughter" and that she was too great a friend of Thomas Seymour.[36] These criticisms made little impression on Kat, but she nevertheless upbraided Seymour for his behaviour and informed the Dowager Queen of what was happening. Katherine Parr ignored Kat's concerns, but when Thomas Seymour again overstepped the bounds of propriety—this time with Elizabeth's consent—Katherine Parr decided to act. One day the Dowager Queen caught her husband while he held Elizabeth in his arms and could not believe her own eyes. In the summer of 1548, Lady Elizabeth was sent away from Katherine's household.

That summer both Anne Seymour and Katherine Parr were heavily pregnant. On 18 July 1548, Edward VI's page, John Fowler, wrote to Thomas Seymour about the outcome of the duchess's delivery: "My Lady of Somerset is brought to bed of a goodly boy, thanks be it to God; and, I trust in almighty God, the Queen's Grace shall have another."[37] On 30 August 1548, the Dowager Queen also gave birth, but not to a son. Thomas immediately penned a letter to his brother Edward, praising his daughter's beauty. She was named Mary after the Lady Mary. The Lord Protector wrote back, addressing his letter to "my very good sister and brother". The letter was couched in the most affectionate terms, but it was underpinned by brotherly rivalry. Although Edward congratulated Thomas on the birth of "so pretty a daughter", he expressed regret that "this, the first" was not a son. Yet the fact that the Dowager Queen had successfully given birth and had a "happy hour", a good delivery, made Edward happy.[38] Yet within days Katherine Parr's health deteriorated, and it soon became apparent that she would succumb to the much-dreaded childbed fever. She died on 5 September 1548.

At the time of the Dowager Queen's death, her relations with the Lord Protector were frosty. She could not get past his "unfriendly parts" and still petitioned him to return her jewels—if not the pieces given to her by Henry VIII, then at least the items she received from her late mother.[39] This was not likely to happen as the Lord Protector had already retrieved some of Katherine's jewels from the King's Jewel House in early 1548, probably for the use of his wife.[40] Yet when Katherine died, Edward and Anne Seymour invited Thomas to their estate and took it upon themselves to help him through the process of grieving. It seemed as if their recent quarrels were buried with Katherine Parr's lifeless body.

At first, Thomas wanted to disband his late wife's royal household and send Lady Jane Grey, his ward, back to her parents. When he regained his composure, however, he decided to keep the girl in his household, where his mother, Margery Seymour, would "be as dear unto the Lady Jane as though she were her own daughter".[41] Thomas had grand plans for Lady Jane Grey and himself—he would marry Lady Elizabeth and try to arrange a marriage between his nephew the King and Jane. He knew that his brother would oppose both schemes since Edward wanted to marry Lady Jane to his eldest son and threatened that if Thomas went after Elizabeth, he would "clap him in the Tower". In a conversation with William Parr, Marquis of Northampton, Thomas predicted that "there would be much ado for my Lady Jane, the Lord Marquis Dorset's daughter; and that my Lord Protector and my Lady Somerset would do what they could to obtain her of my said Lord Marquis for my Lord of Hertford [Edward, their eldest son]".[42] Jane Grey was indeed a great catch; royal and excellently educated, she was perfect wife material for the son of the Lord Protector. Relations between the Seymour brothers deteriorated further when Thomas renewed Katherine Parr's suit for her jewels. In December 1548, he penned a letter to the Lady Mary, beseeching her to write whether she knew if "his Majesty [Henry VIII] gave her Highness [Katherine Parr] the said jewels or did only lend them to her".[43]

Thomas was increasingly critical of his brother, and he was not alone. Edward often made important decisions on state matters without submitting them first to the Privy Council and held meetings with foreign ambassadors without his colleagues present. Thomas desired the young King to break free from under Edward's protectorate and encouraged him to take matters into his own hands. To achieve his ends, Thomas told his nephew that he was but a "beggarly King" who had no money "to play or to give". Edward later admitted that the Lord Protector "dealeth very hardly with me, and keepeth me so straight that I cannot have any money at my will", and he accepted Thomas's gifts of pocket money. At the same time, however, he expressed contentment at how his finances were managed. "Mr Stanhope had [money] for me", he replied to Thomas's criticisms of Somerset. "Mr Stanhope" was Sir Michael Stanhope, the brother of Anne Seymour. He was the chief gentleman of the King's Privy Chamber, keeper of the Privy Purse and controller of the Privy Coffers. The Lord

Protector trusted him above all others and had warm feelings for him as evidenced by one of many letters he wrote to Stanhope, referring to him as "my very loving brother-in-law".[44] Somerset wanted to control access to Edward VI's Privy Chamber by introducing men loyal to him and limiting the influence of others, including his brother. Apart from Stanhope, he also appointed Sir Richard Page, Anne's stepfather. This infuriated Thomas, who resented Page as "so drunken a soul".[45] Thomas knew that whoever guarded the King's person held the power, and, exasperated by his nephew's indecision, he decided to kidnap Edward. On the night of 16 January 1549, just as he was trying to unlock the door leading to the King's bedchamber, Thomas was interrupted by a little dog that started barking furiously at the intruder. One of Edward VI's servants, who slept on a pallet bed in the King's bedchamber, raised an alarm and started shouting, "Help! Murder!" Startled, Thomas fired a shot, killing the King's beloved dog.[46] Thomas's intentions were later blown out of proportion, and soon rumours started circulating at court and abroad that he planned to marry Lady Elizabeth and murder his royal nephew, his brother the Lord Protector, and the King's elder half sister Mary "to make himself King of England".[47] It is possible that he wanted to kidnap

Edward to end the protectorate, but this was not to be. He was arrested on 17 January 1549.

Ten days later, on 27 January, Edward VI's tutor Sir John Cheke wrote an apologetic letter to Anne Seymour. Cheke was eager to ensure the Duchess of Somerset that he still sought her and her husband's patronage after he and his wife incurred the duchess's displeasure. Cheke, a good-natured man who was diligent in his service to Edward VI, was entangled in Thomas Seymour's plot, agreeing to pass £20 from Seymour to the King. Sensing danger, he wisely refused to do more on Thomas's behalf, but passing pocket money was enough to anger the duchess. Perplexed, Cheke wrote:

"Your Grace's singular favour towards me hath always been one of my chief comforts in my diligent service to the King's Majesty, which was the easier to me, because it was well taken; and although in this desert of other men's trouble, and mishap of mine own, I know not precisely of your Grace's favourable goodness towards me, yet I judge that your good Grace's mind towards me, undeserved to be gotten, and undeserved to be lost again, is such that I pass the quieter through the whole course of my danger, and feel the less storm of causeless hap, because I do much stay myself in your Grace's wisdom of taking things truly, and in your goodness of helping the honest favourably."

The "danger" Cheke alluded to was Thomas Seymour's arrest and the extent to which Cheke was involved in his plot. But this was not all. Cheke also apologized for his wife's "misbehaviour" that offended Anne. "My most humble request therefore is, that your Grace's gentleness overcome my wife's faults", he pleaded. Cheke sought to attribute his wife's offence of the duchess to her youth and inexperience, explaining that "in youth there may be pardon where experience lacketh . . . and such we pity, as wisdom cannot be looked for of". Mary Cheke was also pregnant, and Sir John urged Anne to show mercy towards her "for the innocent's sake".[48] In other words, Cheke tried to minimise his wife's faults by implying that she was not only young and foolish, but also hormonal and therefore not to be taken seriously. The King's tutor did not precisely say what his wife's offence was, but the interrogation of Thomas Seymour and his associates offers some clues. Four days before Cheke wrote his letter, Wightman, Thomas's servant, confessed that when his master came to London after Katherine Parr's death, Lady Cheke had "divers conferences" with him at Chelsea Manor. Wightman said:

"At his [Thomas Seymour's] first coming up to London, after the Queen's death, he had (as I heard say) divers conferences with Mrs Cheke at Chelsea, who came from my Lady of Somerset's Grace at Syon tither, only, as Hammond and Pigot told me, to meet with my Lord, and comfort him for the Queen's death, making her excuse to see my Lady Herbert."[49]

Seymour's first visit to London after Katherine Parr's death occurred on 20 September 1548. He stayed at the Dowager Queen's manor at Chelsea, which was being cleared of Katherine's possessions by her sister Anne Herbert, Countess of Pembroke. It appears that Lady Cheke, who stayed with Anne Seymour at Syon House (perhaps as her lady-in-waiting), made several secret trips to Chelsea under the guise of meeting with Lady Herbert, but in reality she was there to talk to Thomas Seymour. Just what they talked about remains unclear, but since Wightman believed Lady Cheke was there to "comfort" Seymour after his wife's death, the Duchess of Somerset may have taken offence at Lady Cheke's behaviour.[50]

Wightman also said that the discord between Thomas Seymour and the Duchess of Somerset occurred because of Katherine Parr: "If ever any grudge were borne towards him by my Lady of Somerset, it was as most men guess for the Queen's cause, who now being taken away by death, it will undoubtedly follow (unless the fault be in himself) that she will bear him as good heart as ever she did in her life."[51]

Thomas Seymour was executed on 20 March 1549. It was the custom to accept one's fate with dignity, mount the scaffold with grace and pray for forgiveness, but Thomas was defiant to the last. It was later revealed that he had two letters addressed to the King's half sisters, urging them to conspire against the Lord Protector, hidden in the soles of his shoes. At the scaffold, he begged for no one's forgiveness, saying merely that the law condemned him:

"I have been brought here to suffer death, for as I was lawfully born into this world so I must lawfully leave it because there is some work to be accomplished which cannot be fulfilled unless I am put out of the way."

He asked the assembled to "pray God of his mercy to receive his soul", then fell to his knees and put his head on the block. It took two strikes of the axe to knock his head off.[52] Hugh Latimer, a Protestant preacher whose sermons were fiery and often controversial, scoffed: "And when a man hath two strokes with an axe, who can tell that between two strokes he doth repent? It is very hard to judge. Well, I will not go so nigh to work, but this I will say, if they ask me what I think of his death: that he died very dangerously, irksomely, horribly."[53]

Among the many accusations against Thomas Seymour, two were very personal in nature. He was accused of having married Katherine Parr "scandalously soon after the death of the King" and of "deceiving the King [Edward VI] and others in persuading them to plead with the Queen, they being already married".[54] These points hardly constituted treason—although the implication was that if the Queen were pregnant by Thomas soon after Henry VIII's death, Thomas would try to foist his child on the throne—and instead seemed to be someone's personal vendetta. Later sources pointed an accusatory finger at Anne Seymour. After he preached a vitriolic sermon condemning Thomas on 19 April 1549, Hugh Latimer complained that there were "some that think and say that I was hired to it and that my Lady of Somerset's Grace hired me to it and that I was her feed man and had money of her to speak it".[55] Latimer denied that he was hired by Anne, but her name was already linked with her brother-in-law's execution. In his *Book of Martyrs*, John Foxe asserted that "many there were, who reported that the Duchess of Somerset had wrought his death", repeating contemporary gossip about Anne's hatred towards Thomas Seymour.[56] In 1630, John Hayward, biographer of Edward VI, further deprecated Anne:

"This woman did bear such invincible hate, first against the Queen Dowager for light causes and woman's quarrels, especially for that she had precedency of place before her, being wife to the greatest Peer in the land, then to the Lord Sudeley for her sake. That albeit the Queen Dowager died by childbirth, yet would not her malice either die or decrease."[57]

Today it is impossible to ascertain whether Anne was in any way involved in Thomas's execution. She may have approved of it, but in the end Thomas was condemned to death by his peers, and many complained about his rash character and inability to work with his brother. Yet Anne also had a personal reason to hate Thomas Seymour. At some point during the nasty family squabble between the Seymour brothers, Thomas sought legal advice concerning his brother's children by his first wife. In 1540, the boys were debarred from succeeding the Lord Protector because of their mother's adultery, but Thomas wondered whether they could be reinstated in their rights and given precedence over Anne's children.[58] This was something that

Anne, a proud and ambitious woman with a forceful personality, would not have forgiven lightly.

In the months following Thomas Seymour's execution, his daughter, Mary, was placed in the nursery at the Somerset household, but it was never Thomas's wish to have his only child raised by a brother whom he loathed. One of Thomas's last wishes was that his daughter would be raised by the Dowager Queen's old friend Katherine Brandon, Duchess of Suffolk. This was a miscalculation on Thomas's part because the Duchess of Suffolk regarded Mary Seymour as an expensive burden. As a daughter of a queen, the seven-month-old infant came to the duchess's household with a large retinue of servants who expected to be paid regular wages. Katherine Brandon was hopelessly in debt and could not afford to house a royal child. She hoped to send Mary Seymour to the late Dowager Queen's relatives, William and Elisabeth Parr, but she was sceptical that they would want to shelter William's niece in their household because their financial situation was almost as difficult as her own: "My Lord Marquis of Northampton, to whom I should deliver her, hath as weak a back for such a burden as I have, and he would receive her, but more willingly if he might receive her with the appurtenances".[59]

The duchess was further irked when she realized that the Lord Protector had failed to keep his promise of providing a pension for his niece. In a letter to William Cecil, Edward Seymour's secretary, Katherine Brandon complained: "I have written to my Lady Somerset at large, which was the let [pity] I wrote not this with mine own hand unto you, and amongst other things for the child, that there may be some pension allotted unto her, according to my Lord's Grace promises." Anne Seymour laboured on behalf of Katherine Parr's daughter since she sent Katherine Brandon a message informing her that "my Lord's grace at her suit had granted certain nursery plate should be delivered with the child".[60] Among the luxurious items belonging to Mary Seymour retrieved from the nursery at the Somerset household were silver pots and goblets, a quilt for the cradle, feather beds, cushions of cloth of gold, wrought stools and other items.

William Cecil, to whom Katherine Brandon wrote, was not in a position to help. Somerset's protectorate was heading towards its abrupt end, and the Lord Protector and Cecil were arrested in the autumn of 1549. But Mary Seymour was eventually restored to her executed father's lands and titles, and in March 1550 the Privy Council granted her money for wages, food and her servants' uniforms. It is often claimed that it was the Lord Protector who made sure that the baby Mary was taken care of, but at that time he was already in disgrace and no longer a member of the Privy Council. Perhaps it was William Parr, condemned by historians for not taking "much interest" in his orphaned niece, who was instrumental in pleading on her behalf with the new regime.[61]

Unfortunately, Mary Seymour died at some point before she reached her second birthday since she was never mentioned in contemporary sources after March 1550. An epitaph written by the Dowager Queen's chaplain reveals that Mary died in her early childhood. In the epitaph, Mary is given her own voice, talking to whoever read the epitaph in first person: "Now, whoever you are, farewell: And because I say no more, you will excuse this by my infancy."[62] She would never come of age and avenge the wrongs done to her father, as Thomas Seymour once hoped, and the Duchess of Somerset would never have to bow to her former rival's daughter.

NOTES

1 John Gough Nichols, *Literary Remains of King Edward the Sixth*, p. xc.
2 Charles Wriothesley, *Wriothesley's Chronicle*, Volume 1, p. 179.
3 *Calendar of State Papers, Spain,* Volume 9, 1547-1549, entry for 7 March 1549.

[4] Ibid., entry for 8 February 1547.
[5] Ibid., entry for 8 February 1549.
[6] D. M. Loades, *Intrigue and Treason: The Tudor Court, 1547-1558*, p. 29.
[7] Janel Mueller, *Katherine Parr: Complete Works and Correspondence*, pp. 131, 135.
[8] Ibid., pp. 134, 138.
[9] Ibid., p. 131.
[10] Ibid., pp. 133-4.
[11] Ibid., p. 141.
[12] Ibid., p. 146.
[13] Agnes Strickland, *Lives of the Queens of England*, Volume 5, p. 163.
[14] *Calendar of State Papers, Domestic Series, of the Reigns of Edward VI, Mary, Elizabeth, 1547-1580*, p. 5.
[15] *Calendar of State Papers, Spain*, Volume 9: 16 June 1547, 10 July 1547.
[16] Jonathan North, *England's Boy King: The Diary of Edward VI, 1547-1553*, p. 21.
[17] John Gough Nichols, *Literary Remains of King Edward the Sixth*, Volume 1, p. cxi.
[18] As pointed out by Margaret Scard in *Edward Seymour: Lord Protector*, p. 149.
[19] *Calendar of State Papers, Spain*, Volume 9: 4 May 1547.
[20] *Correspondance Politique de Odet de Selve, Ambassadeur de France en Angleterre (1546-1549)*, p. 286.
[21] *Chronicle of King Henry VIII of England*, pp. 160-1.
[22] Retha M. Warnicke, *Wicked Women of Tudor England*, pp. 89-90.
[23] *Calendar of State Papers, Spain*, Volume 9: 10 July 1547.
[24] *Chronicle of King Henry VIII of England*, p. 156.
[25] Susan James, *Catherine Parr: Henry VIII's Last Love*, p. 277.
[26] Dakota L. Hamilton, *The Household of Queen Katherine Parr*, pp. 112-3.
[27] Susan James, op. cit.
[28] *Letters and Papers, Henry VIII*, Volume 18 Part 1, n. 66 (39).
[29] Eustace Chapuys originally wrote that the "young creature" was Thomas Wyatt's repudiated wife, but she did not reside at court and was by no means a "young creature" in 1542. Confusion probably arose from the fact that Elisabeth Brooke was the niece of Elisabeth Wyatt, née Brooke. *Calendar of State Papers, Spain*, Volume 6 Part 1, 1538-1542, n. 230. *Letters and Papers, Henry VIII*, Volume 17, n. 92.
[30] Muriel St Clare Byrne, *The Lisle Letters*, Volume 3, p. 378.

[31] William Camden, *The History of the Most Renowned and Victorious Princess Elizabeth*, p. 169.
[32] Gareth Russell, *Young and Damned and Fair: The Life of Catherine Howard, Fifth Wife of King Henry VIII*, p. 238.
[33] *Letters and Papers, Henry VIII,* Volume 20 Part 2, n. 900.
[34] *Calendar of State Papers, Spain,* Volume 9: 23 February 1548.
[35] Samuel Haynes, *A Collection of State Papers, Relating to Affairs in the Reigns of King Henry VIII. King Edward VI, Queen Mary, and Queen Elizabeth from 1542-1570,* p. 99
[36] Ibid.
[37] Janel Mueller, *Katherine Parr: Complete Works and Correspondence*, p. 173.
[38] John Maclean, *The Life of Sir Thomas Seymour*, p. 67.
[39] Janel Mueller, *Katherine Parr: Complete Works and Correspondence*, pp. 168, 170.
[40] SP 10/3 f. 15: 20 January 1548.
[41] *HMC, Salisbury,* p. 55.
[42] Samuel Haynes, *A Collection of State Papers, Relating to Affairs in the Reigns of King Henry VIII. King Edward VI, Queen Mary, and Queen Elizabeth from 1542-1570*, p. 80.
[43] *HMC, Salisbury,* p. 56.
[44] http://www.clivefarahar.com/book/5319/hertford-edward-seymour-earl-of--1500-1552-a-fine-letter-signed-with-a-bold-signature-to-sir-michael-stanhope
[45] Chris Skidmore, *Edward VI: The Lost King of England*, p. 113.
[46] *Calendar of State Papers, Spain,* Volume 9: 27 January 1549.
[47] Ibid., 30 January 1549.
[48] John Strype, *The Life of the Learned Sir John Cheke*, p. 45.
[49] Samuel Haynes, op.cit.
[50] Wightman's confession, however, is ambiguous and can be interpreted in many ways. Historian Elizabeth Norton, for instance, believes that Anne Seymour sent Lady Cheke to Chelsea to offer her condolences and initiate reconciliation with Thomas. Elizabeth Norton, *The Temptation of Elizabeth Tudor*, Kindle edition.
[51] Thomas Fuller, *The Church History of Britain*, Volume 4, p. 77.
[52] Elizabeth Norton, *The Temptation of Elizabeth Tudor*, p. 145.
[53] Stephen Alford, *Edward VI*, p. 42.
[54] William Seymour, *Ordeal by Ambition*, p. 377.
[55] Hugh Latimer, *Secret Sermons*, p. 143.
[56] John Foxe, *The Actes and Monuments of John Foxe: A New and Complete Edition*, p. 283.

---

[57] John Hayward, *The Life and Raigne of King Edward the Sixth*, p. 99.

[58] "A 'Journal' of the Matters of State Happened From Time to Time as Well Within and Without the Realme From and Before the Death of King Edw. the 6th Untill the Yere 1562" in Ian W. Archer's *Religion, Politics, and Society in Sixteenth-Century England*, p. 55.

[59] Janel Mueller, *Katherine Parr: Complete Works and Correspondence*, p. 187.

[60] Ibid., p. 185.

[61] Linda Porter, *Katherine the Queen: The Remarkable Life of Katherine Parr*, p. 341. See also Christine Hartweg's article *Who Cared For Little Mary Seymour's Upkeep? [https://allthingsrobertdudley.wordpress.com/2012/08/13/who-cared-for-little-mary-seymours-upkeep/]*

[62] Janel Mueller, *Katherine Parr: Complete Works and Correspondence*, p. 31.

CHAPTER 5: QUEEN IN ALL BUT NAME

Having served as a lady-in-waiting to all of Henry VIII's wives, during the reign of Edward VI Anne Seymour found herself in the position of a quasi-queen, a great lady of almost regal status. Wives of influential men who served at court often sought employment as the duchess's ladies-in-waiting. Writing in April 1549 to Sir John Thynne, steward of the Lord Protector's household, Thomas Smith, one of the King's principal secretaries, stated that "if my wife can do my Lady's Grace any service, she shall wait as her duty is".[1]

Anne was so influential and her opinion deemed so important that Smith defended his honour against slander in a long and detailed letter to the duchess. In the summer of 1549, he wrote to her denying rumours circulating about him at court.[2] Historically, the Duchess of Somerset has been portrayed as haughty, arrogant and ambitious, and Smith's letter has been often cited as further confirmation of those traits. Yet, as his letter makes clear, it was not the duchess who accused Smith, but his colleagues at court. It is not to say that Anne did not share some of their opinions, however. According to his biographer, Smith "had an arrogant manner, a genius for alienating people, and such insensitivity that he was surprised to discover that acquaintances did not like him".[3] Great lords of the court slandered him for many things, one of the most interesting being that he kept his wife short of funds so that she looked undignified in her shabby clothes. Lady Elizabeth Smith "did not go so gorgeously [apparelled] as some would have her", but it was not because Smith kept her short of funds:

"If that be a fault, although she is little, let her bear it. She hath all my money; I never debarred her of penny, and I have often spoken to her, why she doth not go more courtlike. I never reproved her for bestowing too much of apparel, or anything that should advance her service, or be convenient to her estate. I myself I think should rather be noted to go too sumptuously than otherwise, and therefore, as it is true, so men should judge that I should rather be content she should do so."[4]

Smith's words underline an important truth: one's appearance conveyed an important message about personal wealth and status. King Edward VI himself set the tone for fashion at court; his clothes were dripping with gold, silver and precious stones. François de Scépeaux, a

French diplomat who visited Edward's court twice during his brief reign, noted that the young King made entire chambers sparkle as he moved about his palaces. He had "all his clothes embroidered with gold, silver and pearls", as evidenced by jewels sewn into his clothes and caps.[5]

Anne Seymour was conscious that, as wife of the Lord Protector and aunt of the King, she and her family should express their status through sumptuous clothing. During her time as the Lord Protector's consort, Anne amassed a great amount of clothing and jewellery, as evidenced by her inventories. She wore intricate jewellery including golden chains, ropes of pearls, brooches garnished with rubies and diamonds and rings with precious stones. The Duke and Duchess of Somerset acquired a reputation for acquisitiveness since Anne's husband alone held the keys to five secret treasure rooms at Westminster, and many items were carried to their estates, including a golden circlet made for Anne Boleyn's coronation in 1533 and a sceptre.[6]

Although Edward VI was not married, the wives of his influential statesmen were a visible presence at court. A Florentine visitor, Petruccio Ubaldini, noted that "no banquet is ever given" without ladies being present. He also recorded that:

"The women are by no means inferior in beauty, grace, dress and manners, to the Siennese, or the most admired ladies of Italy. The Lords have a very numerous retinue; a servant generally receives two suits, of little value, in a year, eight crowns, and his board or, instead of the latter, sixpence a day. The people are in general rather tall, but most of the nobles are short, which comes from the custom of marrying rich damsels under age. The men and women are fair, but, to preserve or improve their natural complexion, they are bled two or three times in a year, instead of painting themselves, like the Italian ladies."[7]

Edward's court was very cosmopolitan; he employed Frenchmen, Italians and Spaniards in his retinue, a practice followed by his courtiers, who employed foreigners in their households. Ubladini noted:

"These [foreigners] are much in favour with the courtiers, who like to learn Italian or French, and study the sciences. The rich cause their sons and daughters to study, to learn Latin, Greek, and Hebrew, for since this storm of heresy [Protestantism] has invaded the country, it is considered to be useful to read the Scriptures in the original language."[8]

Anne Seymour's religious zeal and love of learning was well-known at court since she received numerous book dedications between 1548 and 1551. Walter Lynne, who dedicated three books to the duchess, said that she was "known to be (among the noble women of this realm) the most gracious patroness and supporter both of good learning and also of godly men".[9] Her "chief and daily study" of the Scriptures singled her out as the patroness of the reformed religion but also made her a target among conservatives who blamed the Lord Protector for introducing religious reforms, most notably *The Book of Common Prayer* of 1549, "at his wife's instigation".[10] Anne and Edward made sure that their children received excellent educations and employed the leading intellectuals of the period such as Thomas Becon, Nicolas Denisot and William Samuel. Becon believed that "women are the intellectual equals of men" and praised the duke and duchess for providing equal educational opportunities for their sons and daughters.[11]

Three of the Seymour daughters—Anne, Margaret and Jane—were already showing considerable literary skills. On the death of Marguerite de Valois, Queen of Navarre, the girls produced a Latin poem in her honour, earning praise from their contemporaries. Like their mother, Anne the younger and Jane were already corresponding with John Calvin, the French Protestant theologian. In a letter to the teenaged Anne dating to July 1549, Calvin mentioned that "the most illustrious princess, your mother, has lately presented me with a ring as a token of her goodwill".[12]

As first cousins of the King of England, the Seymour children were expected to become the leading luminaries of the next generation of courtiers; Margaret and Jane corresponded with Edward VI in Latin at a very young age while their brother Edward, Earl of Hertford, was among his constant companions.[13] No one could predict that their future, so bright in the beginning of Edward VI's reign, would be ruined by their father's inability to adapt to the expectations of his colleagues on the King's Privy Council.

NOTES

1 J.E. Jackson, *Wiltshire Archaelogical and Natural History Magazine*, Volume 18, p. 261.
2 Thomas Smith to the Duchess of Somerset, July/August 1549. B.L. Harleian MS. 6989, f. 141.
3 Ann B. Clark, *Thought, Word and Deed in the Mid-Tudor Commonwealth : Sir Thomas Smith and Sir William Cecil in the Reign of Edward VI*, p. 35.
4 "Sir Thomas Smith's defence of his conduct and character, addressed to the Duchess of Somerset", *Archealogia*, Volume 38, pp. 120-127.
5 Friedrich von Raumer, *The Political History of England*, p. 115.
6 Jennifer Loach, *Protector Somerset: A Reassessment*, p. 42.

---

[7] Friedrich von Raumer, *The Political History of England*, p. 116.
[8] Ibid., p. 117.
[9] Retha M. Warnicke, *Wicked Women of Tudor England*, p. 99.
[10] *Calendar of State Papers, Spain,* Volume 9, 1547-1549, entry for 10 September 1549.
[11] Thomas Becon, *The Early Works of Thomas Becon*, p. 396
[12] Hastings Robinson, *The Zurich Letters*, Volume 3 Part 2, p. 702.
[13] M.A. Everett Wood, *Letters of Royal and Illustrious Ladies of Great Britain*, p. 199.

CHAPTER 6: SHADOW OF THE TOWER

"Matters in this realm are restless for change", ambassador Van der Delft wrote to Charles V on 15 September 1549. By this time, Edward Seymour's popularity as Lord Protector had dramatically decreased. "The split in the Council is not so well hidden", Van der Delft observed and added that "the ill-feeling between the Protector and the Earl of Warwick is well known".[1] John Dudley, Earl of Warwick, was already plotting his political rival's downfall. Dudley and his colleagues were disenchanted with the way Somerset conducted business. The Lord Protector's most loyal adherent, Sir William Paget, warned him many times over the previous months that he should change his ways. Paget addressed several letters wherein he gently but firmly gave Somerset wise counsel. "When the whole Council shall move you, or give you an advice in a matter" the Protector should "follow the same, and relent sometimes from your opinion". Paget understood that councillors grew annoyed with Somerset's "great choleric fashions, whensoever you are contradicted in that which you have conceived in your head".[2] Somerset was daily growing more authoritarian and made it clear that he felt as if he stood above other councillors, making many decisions without consulting them first. He adopted a royal "we" in his letters, occupied chambers reserved for a royal consort and surrounded the King with men loyal to him. He plunged England into war with Scotland, a war that depleted the royal treasury, and at the same time he seemed oblivious to the country's poor financial state. In the words of the imperial ambassador, Somerset appeared to have had "no care but to build houses for himself and deliver the realm to the enemy".[3] He was referring to the building of Somerset's vast ducal mansion, Somerset Place. It was later insinuated by Somerset's enemies that the he took money from the royal treasury to pay for the work. Somerset's protectorate was heading towards its end as John Dudley brought the discontented councillors together and started plotting his enemy's downfall.

In the last days of September 1549, Edward and Anne were in Hampshire "hunting and sporting", enjoying their last carefree days before the Lord Protector's troubles would begin.[4] In early October, Somerset left Anne at their estate and returned to Hampton Court, where his trusted men were already waiting for him. He summoned his fellow councillors from London, but they tarried for so long that

Somerset started suspecting that "they were brewing something against him" and issued a proclamation ordering the King's "loving subjects" to hasten to Hampton Court and defend Edward VI from a conspiracy. He also despatched messengers with letters to the men he believed could help him, including his brother Sir Henry Seymour, urging them to muster as many armed men as they could. Somerset's bold move was a response to the rumours that the councillors were carrying weapons as they passed through London.

The Lord Protector feared for his wife's safety, and "the duchess was sent for in all haste" on Saturday, arriving from Hampshire after sunset. That night Somerset posted guards around the palace, expecting that the next day he would have to fight with the councillors. At four in the morning, news came from London that some two thousand horsemen were gathering in the city's streets. Somerset immediately rose from his bed and started preparing for the invasion. Hampton Court was a newly refurbished pleasure palace, not prepared to withstand an armed assault, but Somerset ordered the stones paving the courtyards to be dug up and carried to the roof, ready to be hurled down on attackers if they dared to enter. Servants were given orders to join Somerset's army, and even the kitchen boys had weapons thrust into their hands.

The Lord Protector assembled his army and gave a rousing speech to boost their morale. He pointed an accusatory finger at "my Lord of Warwick and certain other lords" who wanted to deprive him of his office and make Lady Mary regent during the King's minority. Somerset invoked the memory of Richard III and reminded the assembled of his usurpation, implying that the lords perhaps sought to destroy Edward VI and not him. In his custody, Somerset continued, Edward was safe: "I do keep him as the apple of my eye; whose health is my comfort and preferment, and whose death is my fall and ruin; and so by all reason I should be as careful of the good preservation of his person as of my own body and soul". Somerset firmly believed that it was his duty to protect the King and proclaimed that he would gladly be the first one to die defending him, to the loud cheers of the assembled. Only the King could deprive him of his office, he said, and invited Edward to address his subjects. The King made a short speech wherein he said "he was displeased that an attempt should be made to take his uncle the Protector away from him, and prayed that all would help him in resisting, for he himself was clothed and ready to arm". Despite the King's backing, it must have been clear to Somerset that he had little support among the Council. Only four loyal men were with him at Hampton Court: Thomas Cranmer, Archbishop of Canterbury, who commanded a private army of sixty men; William Paget, Comptroller of the Royal Household; Thomas Smith and William Petre, the King's secretaries.

Throughout the morning, people flocked to Hampton Court, responding to Somerset's call to arms issued the previous day. Some four thousand peasants armed with crude weapons like pitchforks and scythes marched towards the palace. Captains were appointed to select the most suitable men and send the rest of them away. Meanwhile, ten councillors met at John Dudley's residence at Ely Place. In their record of the events, they blamed Somerset's "ill government" for the recent rebellions and the loss of Haddington and the French forts and reiterated the reasons behind their actions. Somerset was "many times spoken unto both in open Council and otherwise privately" but "refused to give ear to their advices . . . minding to follow his own fantasies". They intended to open "friendly communication . . . about the reformation of the state" with him on Sunday, 5 October, but heard by credible reports that the Lord Protector was gathering an army to fight with them.

Both sides were preparing for bloodshed. Somerset sent Edward Wolf, member of the Privy Chamber, "secretly to take the Tower of London", but the fortress had already fallen into the hands of the councillors. The King also sent Sir William Petre to London, conveying bitter accusations, but the councillors retained him with them, to Edward VI's astonishment. Somerset was becoming increasingly worried and decided to send his wife to the safety of her half brother's house at Beddington in Surrey before removing the King and what remained of his court to Windsor Castle.

Beddington Place was steeped in royal history. This "paradise of pleasure" originally belonged to Henry VIII's Master of the Horse, Sir Nicholas Carew (executed in 1539), and was used by the King as a romantic retreat when he courted his mistresses. It was here that Anne Boleyn was briefly lodged during the visit of papal legate in November 1528. Eight years later it was another of the King's mistresses, Jane Seymour, who stayed there in May 1536 awaiting news of her rival's trial, most likely accompanied by her sister-in-law.[5]

Anne was devastated and "went out weeping". On her way to Beddington, she was "very badly handled in words by the courtiers and peasants, who put all this trouble down to her". Indeed, a pamphlet about Somerset's fall castigated Anne as "that imperious and insolent woman his wife". It was Anne's "ambitious wit and mischievous persuasions", the tract continued, that "led him and directed him", not only in private matters, but "even also in the weighty affairs and government of the realm to the great harm and dishonour of the same and to the more great peril of the King our sovereign lord's estate".[6] Anne was not only her husband's beloved spouse, but also his confidante. She was no shrinking violet and was not afraid to take a stance about religion and politics. Somerset apparently respected his wife's opinions and often consulted her about important matters, as evidenced by an interesting exchange between William Paget and the imperial ambassador in August 1549.

When Van der Delft informed Paget during one of their secret meetings that he "considered him personally to blame for all the evil that had befallen this kingdom, since he had been the principal instrument in setting us up a Protector who would certainly never do any good", Paget defended himself by saying that the Lord Protector had a "bad wife", implying that Somerset listened too much to Anne. "I rejoined that that amounted to a confession of his unworthiness, since he allowed himself to be ruled by his wife", the ambassador concluded.[7] It was Paget's clumsy attempt at exonerating Somerset by blaming Anne for his bad decisions. But Paget, Somerset's loyal adherent, knew well that the Lord Protector was entirely to blame. Exasperated by Somerset's inaction after a series of his kindly advices, Paget later described himself as Cassandra, the ancient prophetess who foresaw the destruction of Troy but was believed by no one.

Whether Anne knew that Paget castigated her as Somerset's "bad wife" or not, she decided to seek his help. As soon as she reached her half brother's estate at Beddington in Surrey, she sat down to compose a letter to Paget, whom she praised as a man of "great wisdom and friendly nature". She hoped that Paget, who always stood by her husband's side, would help. "I know you may do much good in these matters being a wise man", she wrote. Anne believed that Somerset was framed because she knew he was innocent of the charges laid against him. These charges were so "untrue and most unfriendly" that she believed that "some wicked person or persons" sought her beloved husband's destruction. "Good Master Comptroller, comfort my Lord as I trust you do, both with council and otherwise, for I much fear he is sore grieved at the heart", Anne beseeched him.[8]

Paget was in the royal entourage when Somerset crept away under the cover of darkness from Hampton Court to Windsor Castle. It was a hasty flight, and the King later complained that he felt the move was unnecessary. When Edward VI moved between his palaces, word was usually sent in advance for his servants to bring furniture, sweep the palaces clean, light fires and arrange for food supplies from the local farmers. A royal progress was usually planned for such occasions so that the King could be seen by his subjects, who lined the streets to greet him as he passed. This time, however, Edward came under the cover of darkness to cold, bare walls and caught a chill on his way to Windsor. "Methinks I am in prison; here be no galleries nor no gardens to walk in", he complained. Somerset was later accused of removing "the King's Majesty's person late in the night from Hampton Court to Windsor, without any provision there made for his Grace, whereby his Highness was not only in great fear, but took also such disease as was to his great peril".[9] The councillors in London, fearing that their sovereign would be deprived of food, sent necessary provisions together with assurances of their good intentions.

Somerset was well aware that he could be accused of high treason and imprisoned in the Tower. He knew only too well what would happen to the riches he amassed over the years if he should be found guilty: greedy courtiers would put forward their claims for his clothes, plate, vestments from his private chapel and everything else. After all, he himself had selected rich pickings from the estates of the Duke of Norfolk, accused of treason in 1546. As he lingered at Windsor with the King, exchanging letters with the councillors in London, Somerset ordered his servants to spirit his goods out of his properties at Syon and Sheen and move them to their own houses. "Coffers and other stuff" were transported to Beddington in Surrey (house of Michael Stanhope) and to the houses of Somerset's household officers: Richard Davy, porter; Walter Blackwell, footman; William Hatfield, yeoman of the scullery; and Rutur and William Smith, carters. In the morning on Monday, 7 October, Anne was also seen carrying "with her openly in the sight of people four square caskets" and stopping with them at the house of Richard Whalley at Wimbledon.[10]

Somerset started to realise how isolated he was and how futile it was to fight with his fellow councillors. He wrote to them, admitting defeat and assuring that he never intended to harm any of them. To safeguard himself from possible attacks, Somerset made sure that the King included his own letter, urging them to treat his uncle with respect. Sir Philip Hoby, a well-liked and respected ambassador and courtier, met with Somerset and the King at Windsor and acted as a go-between, carrying messages to and fro. One of the letters was addressed to John Dudley, wherein Somerset wondered why, after such a long friendship, Dudley turned his back on him, but asked that the two remain friends. Somerset's *coup d'etat,* as it was later known, ended with his incarceration in the Tower.

Fearing that Edward Seymour faced imminent execution, Anne decided to ally herself with her husband's political opponent. The man who engineered Seymour's arrest was John Dudley, Earl of Warwick, the Lord Protector's erstwhile political partner and supporter. He was the son of Henry VII's financial minister, Edmund Dudley, who had been executed during the early reign of Henry VIII. His father's execution was not an impediment to Dudley's career; he was knighted in 1523 and by 1533 he had been made Master of the Armoury in the Tower of London. He served as Master of the Horse in Anne of Cleves's household in 1540, and three years later was created Viscount Lisle, when this title fell into abeyance after Arthur Plantagenet's death.[11] In 1543, he became Lord Admiral and later that year joined the Privy Council and was elected as a member of the Order of the Garter. Henry VIII was fond of John Dudley and made him an executor to his last will in 1547, leaving him a substantial legacy of £500.

Early in Edward VI's reign, the imperial ambassador Van der Delft noted that a clash between the Lord Protector and the Earl of Warwick was inevitable. "It is, of course, quite likely that some jealousy or rivalry may arise between the Earl of Hertford and the Lord Admiral", he wrote in February 1547, adding that the two men were "widely different in character". The ambassador's description throws light on their respective characters as seen through the eyes of a foreign diplomat:

"[T]he Lord Admiral being of high courage will not willingly submit to his colleague. He is, moreover, in higher favour both with the people and with the nobles than the Earl of Hertford, owing to his liberality and splendour. The Protector, on the other hand, is not so accomplished in this respect, and is indeed looked down upon by everybody as a dry, sour, opinionated man."[12]

John Dudley received the earldom of Warwick in the same ceremony that saw Edward Seymour become Duke of Somerset in February 1547. He also relinquished the admiralty and became Lord Great Chamberlain. Rumour had it that Dudley had long sought the opportunity to curb the Lord Protector's influence and bring him down. According to some sources, it was Dudley who convinced the Lord Protector to send his brother to the scaffold in 1549, knowing full well that fratricide could cost the Lord Protector his popularity among the people. Shortly after Thomas Seymour's execution, an anonymous author wrote how Dudley "feared much the amity between the two brethren, the Duke of Somerset [and] Sir Thomas Seymour" and had sought "with all diligence to understand their humours; and so little by little to compass them both". Dudley took the Lord Protector's side in the quarrel between the brothers and was a frequent guest at Somerset House, where he stayed "for as long as Sir Thomas Seymour lived . . . always at hand" until after Seymour's execution, when Dudley moved to his own residence.[13] Whatever the truth behind Dudley's involvement in Thomas Seymour's execution, , in the autumn of 1549 Edward Seymour's influence was on the wane, and it looked like he could be executed for treason.

Anne Seymour decided to explore her friendship with Dudley's wife to her best advantage. Jane Dudley, Countess of Warwick, was the daughter of Edward

Guildford and his first wife, Eleanor West, daughter of Thomas West, Lord de la Warr. Jane was raised and educated with John because in 1512 her father gained wardship of the young John Dudley. The couple were married by late 1525 or early 1526; their first son, Henry, was born in 1526. Arranged marriages were customary among Tudor nobility, and they were often unhappy matches. Yet the Dudleys appear to have been a loving and harmonious couple who fostered a large family of thirteen children—eight sons and five daughters. Frequent childbearing did not bar Jane from a career as a lady-in-waiting to Henry VIII's queens. Lady Dudley's court career started in the early 1530s when she was recorded among the ladies-in-waiting who presented New Year's gifts to Henry VIII. Jane was recorded as a "young lady Guildford" to distinguish her from her grandmother, the illustrious Jane Vaux Guildford, a seasoned lady-in-waiting who served in the households of Elizabeth of York, Katharine of Aragon and Mary the French Queen. Jane's name was again recorded in the New Year's gift list in 1534, strengthening the notion that she served as Anne Boleyn's lady-in-waiting. Like most ladies at court, Jane swiftly transferred to the household of Jane Seymour and took part in the Queen's funeral procession on 12 November 1537. During the three-year period of Henry VIII's widowhood, Lady Dudley served as lady-in-waiting to the King's daughter Mary, a connection that would prove crucial later in Jane's life. When the King briefly married Anne of Cleves in January 1540, Lady Dudley was among her ladies. She did not serve in the household of Katherine Howard, but resumed her role as lady-in-waiting to the King's sixth wife, Katherine Parr and became an influential member of her Privy Chamber.

Just like Anne Seymour, Jane was a reformer, and her name came up when the conservative faction tried to purge the court of heretics in 1546. Unlike Anne, however, Jane was not "very bold before women" and was not prominent at court during the Seymour protectorate, although her influence on her husband was recognized by contemporaries.[14] Her poor health may have been one of the reasons why she was disinclined to take up a more visible role at court. In 1548, for instance, her husband reported that she "had had her fit again more extreme that she had any time yet", suggesting that she suffered from bouts of ill health.[15]

The Seymours and Dudleys were not strangers. They knew each other from their service in the households of

Henry VIII and his wives, a service that spanned two decades. There exists evidence that they were not only colleagues but also friends. In 1537, a servant of John Dudley "brought my Lady a picture of Queen Jane" and two years later "my Lady Dudley" and her husband were among eminent guests who joined the Seymours during supper.[16]

In early December 1549, Anne "went to my Lord of Warwick and spoke with my Lady [his wife]".[17] The imperial ambassador Van der Delft observed that "the Earl of Warwick, who is a very changeable and unstable person" began to show favour to Edward Seymour because he "has been won over by the Protector's wife, who is always in his house".[18]

Just what conversations took place between Anne and the Dudleys after Somerset was arrested are hinted at in the contemporary *Spanish Chronicle*.[19] Its anonymous author encapsulated Anne's character in the following sentence: "The wife of the Protector was . . . a very prudent woman, and saw that she would have to humble herself." When she reached the house of the Dudleys, she threw herself on her knees in front of the Earl of Warwick and said:

"My lord, I am much surprised that there should have been words which have angered you, between my husband and yourself, for I always heard him say that the King had no wiser or more prudent councillor in his realm than you, and yet out of mere passion you have had him proclaimed a traitor; an act of which neither God nor man can think well. It lies in your hands to make amends, and as he has done no treason, I pray you consider that he is the King's uncle, and although the King is too young to understand yet, he will, nevertheless, in time come to know the truth, if you, my lord, are the cause of my husband's death."

Dudley certainly felt awkward during Anne's speech as he tried to raise her from her knees, "and it was more by force than with her will that at last he made her sit on a chair". With Anne seated, he told her that he was the reason her husband was made Lord Protector in the first place and that "the kingdom has never been so ruined as it is now, and yet it is confidently asserted that he has spent more than two hundred thousand ducats in his buildings, which seems almost incredible". "Where can he have got these sums if not out of the King's treasure?" Dudley enquired of Anne, telling her plainly that "for want of money we have lost the forts at Boulogne, which cost a treasure to erect, as well as other important things in Scotland, all through his penuriousness, and his desire to take the treasure for himself, instead of providing properly. For the least of these things he deserves death". Anne did not address these charges directly as she knew there was a ring of truth to them. Instead, she said:

"My lord, it has not been so much the Duke's fault as you attribute to him, and I beg you, putting aside anger, and for fellowship's sake, to be a good friend to him, for I well know that if you are for him none will be against him."

Dudley's anger softened, and he promised Anne that he would do his best to help the disgraced Protector. Anne "did not like to press him further" but asked if she could talk to Dudley's wife. The two women "talked for a long time" in Jane Dudley's private chambers, and Anne begged Jane to "speak that night to her husband in favour of the Duke". Jane promised she would, and Anne gave her "a very rich jewel of diamonds" to remind her of the promise made. At first, Jane refused to take it but in the end agreed.

The next day Anne returned and begged Dudley to let her visit her husband in the Tower; Dudley replied that he would ask the Privy Council. "Great is the power of gifts", mused the chronicler, letting the readers know that Lady

Dudley spoke on the Duke of Somerset's behalf and gave her husband the rich piece of jewellery she received from Anne. Dudley allowed Anne the freedom to visit her husband as often "as she pleased", and she went once a day to the Tower.[20] A visit she paid the Lord Protector on Christmas Day 1549 was recorded; her visit was "to his no little comfort".[21]

Anne continued her efforts on Edward's behalf, and in January 1550 the imperial ambassador reported that "the said Warwick, who has succeeded in gaining full control of affairs, is openly favourable to the Protector, and their wives exchange banquets and festivities daily".[22] Yet Anne still worried about Edward's fate since the Earls of Arundel and Southampton called for his head, and in late January 1550 she was reportedly "somewhat acrased [distraught]" and closeted herself away at her rented apartments in the Savoy Palace.[23]

On 6 February 1550, Edward Seymour was released from the Tower, thanks largely to Anne's efforts. He was taken by the Lieutenant of the Tower to the Sheriff of London's house, where he met with John Dudley and the entire Council. The imperial ambassador reported:

"The Council dined there, and all were assembled together, when the Protector, accompanied by a few gentlemen, entered the room and bowed to them, keeping his head uncovered, and receiving no sign from any of them until after he was shown certain letters patent which presumably were the King's pardon, as he took them and gave thanks to the King for his mercy, and the gentlemen of the Council for their favour."[24]

After meeting with the councillors, Edward "took his barge and passed to Savoy [Palace] where my Lady his wife lied and hath kept her chamber for a long time", reported an eyewitness.[25] The couple moved to their property at Syon, the former site of the principal monastery of the Bridgettine order, located in Twickenham Park on the Thames. The Seymours built one of their homes, Syon House, in the Italian Renaissance style there. Edward lost his title of Lord Protector but was still a respected member of Edward VI's regime. On 3 June 1550, the Seymour-Dudley alliance was confirmed when Edward Seymour's eldest daughter, Anne, married John Dudley's eldest son, John, Viscount Lisle. "It is said that the two mothers have made the match", observed the new imperial ambassador, Jehan Scheyvfe.[26] Yet despite Anne Seymour's and Jane

Dudley's efforts to reconcile their husbands, neither of the women were prominent during the wedding ceremony.

Elisabeth Parr, Marchioness of Northampton, eclipsed these two powerful female players. During the banquet celebrating the Seymour-Dudley match hosted by the French ambassador François de Vendôme, Vidame de Chartres, she received an enamelled chain worth two hundred crowns. The other ladies, including three daughters of Anne and Edward, received presents of lesser value, "each one according to her station". Vendôme "did not take particular notice of anyone except of the Duke of Somerset and the Marchioness of Northampton"; he talked to them through an interpreter.[27] The status of Elisabeth and her husband was raised after William, disillusioned with Edward Seymour's hostile stance towards his marriage to Elisabeth, joined John Dudley's plot to overthrow the Lord Protector and was rewarded for his loyalty, becoming Lord Chamberlain of England on 2 February 1550.

Although Edward Seymour was not restored to his position of Lord Protector, he was still a visible presence at court and an influential member of the Privy Council. Yet he could not come to terms with his degradation and was desperate to claw his way back to the pinnacle of power. Tensions between Dudley and Seymour intensified in April 1551, when the imperial ambassador reported that "the Duke and my Lord of Warwick fell into a dispute in open Council, but the matter was soon calmed down". Later that month, on St George's Day, Dudley made sure that the words "on his mother's side" were inserted when Somerset's title of "uncle to the King of England" was read out loud.[28] In October 1551, Dudley was created Duke of Northumberland and made a decisive move against Somerset, accusing him of planning to murder his fellow councillors and trying to avenge himself for his previous imprisonment. Somerset and his associates were arrested on 17 October 1551. Jehan Scheyfve, imperial ambassador, reported what he heard from William Cecil, Somerset's former secretary, now secretary to the King:

"When I arrived, Secretary Cecil acted as spokesman and gave me the following account of the occurrence that had moved the Council to send for me. One of the foremost and most distinguished of their body, the Duke of Somerset, had laid aside all fear of God, all reverence and duty towards his Sovereign and natural Lord, and plotted to seize the Tower of London, and consequently the royal treasury and military stores there kept, in order to subdue the town. Moreover, he had endeavoured to have several other castles and forts, particularly in the North Country, surprised and occupied by his accomplices, and also to rouse the commons and peasantry to revolt, thus jeopardising the King's person and his country's welfare without the slightest excuse or reason. Not content with this, he had turned his back on all honour and humanity and conceived a plan to invite his colleagues of the Council to a banquet to have them struck down and murdered by hired assassins; which seemed to them a very horrible action, and calculated to give a very evil example. The Council, warned of their danger, had been able to arrest the Duke and some of his party without any scandal or disturbance."[29]

During his trial that took place on 1 December 1551, Somerset "confessed that he had talked with some of his familiars and friends about finding means to abase the Duke of Northumberland, but not to kill him".[30] Among Somerset's most notable co-conspirators was Thomas Arundel, who hotly denied planning to murder Northumberland and other councillors, but confessed to secret talks with Somerset about calling Dudley and his cronies to "answer and reform things". Indeed, they discussed "the reformation and the estate of the realm" and agreed that John Dudley and his most loyal adherent, William Parr, should be sent to the Tower. Yet Somerset, perhaps realising the futility of such plans, lost interest in the plot and told his servant William Crane that he "would no further meddle with the apprehension of any of the Council". He also urged Crane to tell the Duchess of Somerset to "bade her bid M. Stanhope to meddle no more in talk" with Arundel.[31] Anne, it appears, was fully involved in plans for restoring her husband to his former position. She was so confident that she was heard saying to her friends that "she hoped the world might soon change, and that her husband, who was now very low and in debt, might someday be in a position to do something for those who wished him well".[32] When Dudley learned of Anne's involvement, he decided to lock her up in the Tower. Soon after Anne's arrest the imperial ambassador reported:

"Some say that they [councillors] have already found enough material to proceed upon, and even that Somerset and his wife have owned up to the conspiracy; though others think his enemies have started the rumour. Still, as far as I am able to ascertain, they are finding some matter; and they will not omit to bring up the story of his former imprisonment against the Duke. It seems that God wishes to punish him and his wife, as they were the instruments of the introduction of the new religion into England."[33]

Thomas Norton, secretary to the Duke of Somerset, wrote to John Calvin that Anne, who was "guarded with great care" in the Tower, was not charged with anything. He added that he was "ignorant as to what offence she is suffering". Since no formal charges were brought against her, Norton believed that Anne "was not imprisoned for having committed a crime, but to prevent her from committing one".[34] The King devoted a short space in his *Chronicle* to his aunt, noting that "the duchess, Crane and his wife, with their chamber's keeper were sent to the Tower for devising these treasons".[35]

During the interrogation of witnesses, it was revealed that Somerset planned to marry his daughter Jane to the King. Edward VI, who took a lively interest in his uncle's trial, recorded in his *Chronicle*:

"The Lord Strange confessed how the duke willed him to stir me to marry his third daughter the lady Jane, and willed him to be his spy in all matters of my doings and sayings, and to know when some of my council spoke secretly with me. This he confessed himself."[36]

Henry Stanley, Lord Strange, was the King's companion and friend, and he had been approached by Somerset, who wanted to have a spy in the King's private apartments. He was brought to Somerset's trial and confirmed that the duke asked him to persuade the King to marry his daughter; the charge was particularly damning as Edward VI's councillors were negotiating a French marriage for the young King. Somerset encouraged Lord Strange to make the King "believe that it would be better for the country's sake if he married within the kingdom". To make Lord Strange more willing to do his bidding, Somerset promised to marry him to another daughter of his; he had four unmarried girls at the time. The charge appears to have been true, as Somerset defended himself by saying that "history showed that the Kings of England had usually married in the country and that he would have done nothing without the Council's consent". Only fourteen at the time, Edward VI wanted to be nobody's pawn. "It appears that this matter of the marriage was the principal reason why the Duke lost the King's favour", observed the imperial ambassador.[37]

Somerset entered Westminster Hall for his trial amid large crowds chanting, "God Save the Duke." He was still popular with the masses who had gathered outside, awaiting the final verdict. The imperial ambassador noted that the crowds were so numerous and stirred up that "it was feared that some commotion might ensue".[38] Somerset defended himself admirably and was proclaimed innocent of high treason. The King did not attend his uncle's trial in person but scrupulously noted all of its proceedings in his diary and wrote about it in copious detail to his friend Barnaby Fitzpatrick. Historians believe that Edward VI was fed information about the trial by Northumberland and his crew. Indeed, although Somerset denied that he wanted to kill Northumberland and other councillors, Edward seemed to believe his uncle had confessed to it. Northumberland told the young King that he would not allow that attempt on his life be regarded as an act of treason—as indeed it was not since he wasn't a member of the royal family. Yet Somerset was found guilty of a felony and sentenced to be hanged. When the sentence was read out, Somerset "begged the Council to intercede with the King to obtain a pardon for him".[39] The King's version, preserved in his diary, was more dramatic: "He gave thanks to the lords for the open trial, and cried mercy of the Duke of Northumberland, Marquis of Northampton and the Earl of Pembroke for his ill meaning against them, and made suit for his life, wife and children, servants and debts."[40]

It was customary for the accused to be escorted to the Tower with an axe turned towards them if they had been found guilty of treason. Since Somerset was cleared of this charge, he was escorted, as Edward VI noted, "without the axe".[41] Crowds who gathered outside Westminster Hall mistakenly believed that their beloved "Good Duke" had been proclaimed innocent of all the charges and threw their caps in the air as a sign of jubilation, shouting with joy. The tumult was so loud that the King heard it and asked "what it meant". "When he was told that the Duke of Somerset had been acquitted, he said he had never believed Somerset could be a traitor", wrote the imperial ambassador.[42] Edward appeared somewhat more unconcerned in his diary, writing, with a palpable note of annoyance, that: "The people, knowing not the matter, shouted half a dozen times, so loud that from the hall door it was heard at Charing Cross plainly, and rumours went that he was quit of all."[43]

Many believed that the sentence of hanging would not be carried out since Somerset threw himself on the King's mercy, and Edward VI was known to pardon prisoners accused of felonies every day. A sense that the trial was rigged by Northumberland and his cronies permeated the court and streets of London. Many questioned whether the Duke of Northumberland, the

Marquis of Northampton and the Earl of Pembroke should even sit at Somerset's trial since many charges concerned them directly. How could they judge Somerset without bias? Indeed, all three were said to have been desperate to see Somerset's head roll. Northumberland was particularly vicious in pursuing his vendetta against Somerset, as he made sure that a special act was passed in the previous Parliament, classifying gathering men with the intention of imprisoning or killing a member of the Privy Council as high treason. William Parr, Marquis of Northampton, and William Herbert, Earl of Pembroke, were also far from impartial. Pembroke was married to Northampton's sister, Anne Parr, and the two were close friends. They were also still mourning after the execution of their brother-in-law and friend, Thomas Seymour, and blamed Somerset for it. Now an opportunity to avenge him presented itself, and they were eager to grasp it with both hands.

Although the imperial ambassador reported that he heard that the Duke of Somerset was not well treated in the Tower, this was far from the truth. As the King's relatives, Edward and Anne Seymour were lodged in comfortable confinement. Each had servants to tend to their daily needs; the duke had four attendants, the duchess three.[44] Both also requested fine clothing and plate to be brought from their estates. Somerset "prayed to have" such things as a velvet cap, nightcap, two pairs of velvet shoes, two doublets, three shirts, as well as his own tablecloths, napkins and towels. Anne ordered such items as a velvet waistcoat, two pairs of knitted hose, one pair of woollen hose, seven newly made "plain smocks", seven high-collared partlets with detachable ruffs, a gown of black velvet edged with genet fur, two pairs of gloves and leather slippers. It is also clear that the duchess wanted to pass her time in reading and sewing. She had three "little books covered with black velvet" delivered to her and also "some black silk and white thread".[45]

As Edward and Anne awaited further news as to their fates, the court immersed itself in a series of splendid Christmas festivities. "During these last feasts held at Greenwich the King kept open Court and table, which had not yet been done in his time", reported imperial ambassador Jehan Scheyfve. "Many jousts, tourneys and other sports were also held for his Majesty's pleasure and recreation", he wrote before ominously adding that they were devised by Northumberland and his supporters to distract Edward VI from thinking about his uncle. Not that he objected to any of this. Again, the young King's writings offer a window into his thoughts. "This last Christmas hath been well and merrily passed", he wrote to Barnaby Fitzpatrick. An entry in the King's diary also shows that he was preoccupied with entertainments, noting how, on 3 January 1552, eighteen men—including the Duke of Northumberland's three sons—jousted and "accomplished their courses right well".[46] By 19 January, the fun and games were all over; that day the King wrote his uncle a letter, wherein he informed him that he commuted the sentence from hanging to a more merciful beheading by an axe. Somerset accepted his fate and, touchingly, scribbled a note in his book "the day before my death", submitting himself to God.

On the morning of 22 January 1552 he was escorted by an armed guard to the Tower Hill, where a multitude of people gathered to witness his last moments despite a curfew imposed on the Londoners for this occasion. Climbing the steps of the scaffold, Somerset knelt and commended himself to God before addressing the sea of faces. He acknowledged that he had been condemned by law to die and he accepted his fate, but a note of bitterness crept into his speech when he said that "I never offended against the King, neither by word nor deed, and have been always as faithful and as true unto the realm as any man hath been". Somerset knew that his death had been engineered by Northumberland, but this mattered but little at that moment. It was now left to him to repent for his sins, pray to God for forgiveness and hope for as quick a stroke of an axe as possible. But then, as Somerset was still addressing the crowds, a great noise was heard, described by onlookers as sounding like a powerful explosion of gunpowder. Chaos ensued, and the people started running in all directions, throwing themselves upon the ground and into nearby ditches. It soon dawned on them that it was the sound of large crowds from nearby hamlets, running late for the execution. Then another distraction occurred; one Sir Anthony Browne rode towards the scaffold, and many believed he carried a last-minute pardon from the King. The people erupted in praise and rejoicing, exclaiming, "Pardon, pardon is come, God save the King!" But it was not so. During all this tumult, the Duke of Somerset stood still on the scaffold, astonished but calm. "Dearly beloved friends, there is no such matter here in hand as you vainly hope or believe", he addressed them again and continued his speech, beseeching the masses to calm down. "I pray you all be quiet and without tumult, for I am even now quiet . . . For albeit the spirit be willing and ready, the flesh is frail and wavering and through your quietness, I shall be much more the quieter".[47] After his speech ended, Somerset knelt down and prayed from a scroll given to him by a priest. He then stood up and bade farewell to each man standing on the scaffold, "taking them all by the hands". This done, the duke turned to the executioner and paid for what he hoped would be a clean stroke of the axe. He then knelt in the straw and untied his shirt, baring his neck and arms, and blindfolded himself with a handkerchief. It took one "heavy stroke of the axe" to end his life, "to the lamentable sight and grief of thousands that heartily praised God for him, and entirely loved him".[48] Somerset's lifeless body was unceremoniously thrown into a cart and "buried irreverently and without anyone being present" in the Chapel of St Peter ad Vincula in the Tower.[49]

"The Duke of Somerset is deeply mourned by the people, who are far from satisfied with his execution, when he had only been convicted of felony", wrote the imperial ambassador Jehan Scheyfve. Those who could come near the spot where he was put to death "washed their hands in his blood and others dipped their handkerchiefs in it".[50] "The Duke of Somerset had his head cut off upon Tower hill between eight and nine o'clock in the morning", according to an arid note in the King's diary.[51] Edward VI has been criticized by historians for this seeming lack of emotion when describing Somerset's execution, but the imperial ambassador heard a rumour that suggested otherwise:

"It is said that, at first, the King was not disposed to consent to Somerset's execution, but agreed after the French ambassador had used certain persuasive arguments, showing him that an example was required in so serious a matter, that many disturbances had cropped up in the kingdom during Somerset's administration and protectorate, and, above all, that he was so popular that the commons had become less devoted to the Crown."[52]

In his 1630 biography of Edward VI, John Hayward wrote that whenever somebody spoke about Somerset, the King "would often sigh and let fall tears", sometimes saying that his uncle "had done nothing that deserved death, or if he had, that it was very small, and proceeded rather from his wife than from himself".[53] Hayward's words, however, should be read with extreme caution. His description of Anne Seymour's character was so vicious that it prompted her nineteenth-century biographer to conclude that "no one, certainly, was ever more grossly slandered than was Anne Duchess of Somerset by Hayward".[54] According to Hayward, Anne was "a woman for many imperfections intolerable, but for pride monstrous . . . exceeding both subtle and violent in accomplishing her ends, for which she spurned over all respects both of conscience and of shame". When describing Anne's arrest, Hayward went as far as to say that "no man [was] grieving thereat because her pride and baseness of life overbalanced all pity". He blamed Anne for all "mischief" that he believed proceeded from "her wicked working brain".[55]

Hayward's misogyny aside, he was writing at the time when Somerset was a Protestant hero lauded as the "good Duke" in John Foxe's *Book of Martyrs*. Edward VI never made an official statement on his uncle's death, but in post-Edwardian England many felt he should have. His speech in Hayward's work presents a boy who credited rumours ("Alas how falsely have I been abused? How weekly carried? How little was I master of mine own judgment, that both his death and the envy there of must be laid upon me.") and who chose to blame a woman for Somerset's failings.[56]

After her husband's death, Anne, still secluded in the Tower, firmly believed that she would follow him to the scaffold. Only days after his execution she requested the Bishop of Gloucester visit her "for the settling of her conscience".[57] On 12 February 1552, the imperial ambassador noted that people widely believed that she "will soon go the same way".[58] This was not to happen, but the duchess remained a prisoner in the Tower. Anne Seymour's life behind the Tower's walls was relatively comfortable. The Privy Council allotted £100 of revenue out of her late husband's lands for her upkeep and allowed her to keep two gentlewomen and her own cook. Her mother, the widowed Lady Page, was "for the most part with the said duchess" and moved in with Anne to take care of her.[59]

Edward Seymour was not the only casualty of the Duke of Northumberland's plans. Among the Duke of Somerset's adherents who were said to abet him in his plotting were Sir Thomas Arundel, Sir Myles Partridge, Sir Ralf Fane and Anne's half brother, Sir Michael Stanhope. On 22 February 1552, the Privy Council informed them that "they should against Friday next prepare themselves to die according to their condemnations".[60] Their executions took place on Friday, 23 February. Anne's sister-in-law, the widowed Lady Stanhope, lost Beddington Place, and the Privy Council made necessary arrangements to discharge her household, pay her servants their wages and "provide her of an other house".[61]

With the Duke of Somerset dead and his wife incarcerated in the Tower, the Seymour children were deprived of the company of both of their parents and had no right to claim their father's titles and possessions. The imperial ambassador heard rumour that they were to be proclaimed bastards "because it seems that Somerset's widow had been promised to a certain gentleman before the Duke married her".[62] Nothing came of these plans, but an Act of Parliament restored Somerset's elder son of his first marriage to some of his mother's possessions sold by Somerset without her assent. Again, Anne was blamed for Somerset's earlier decision to deprive his sons of their inheritance.[63]

Necessary provisions were made for the Seymour children. Their eldest daughter, Anne, was married to John Dudley's son and was thus well taken care of. The other four girls—Margaret, Jane, Mary and Catherine—were unmarried and placed in the household of their paternal aunt, the recently widowed Elizabeth Cromwell, who received four hundred marks per year for their upkeep from the King. The youngest daughter, two-year-old Elizabeth, was placed in the household of their other paternal aunt, Dorothy Smith, who was also widowed and who also received one hundred marks yearly to maintain her niece. The boys—Edward, Henry and another Edward—were residing in the household of William Paulet, Marquis of Winchester, and became the King's wards.[64]

Taking care of her nieces proved trying for Elizabeth Cromwell, who already had five of her own children. In a letter to William Cecil, Lady Cromwell wrote that since she was "now a lone woman", she could not take care of her four nieces. She continued:

"Wherefore, considering with myself the weighty burden and care which nature bindeth me to be mindful of, as well for the bestowing of my own children, as also for such poor family as my late lord and husband hath left me unprovided for, enforceth me to require your help and advice, that hereafter, about Christmas next, or shortly after then, by your good means, my said honourable lords of the Council may understand that, when my said nieces have accomplished a full year with me, then my trust is that they shall be otherwhere provided for and bestowed than with me: trusting that there be places enough where they may be, better than with me; and, as I do perceive by them many ways, much more to their own contentations and pleasings. And even as I was bold to write unto the King's highness's most honourable Council, that I, being a lone woman, not nigh any of my kinsfolk, whereby I the rather am destitute of friendly advice and counsel, how to use myself in the rule of such company as now I am careful of, so now I am likewise bold to declare the same unto you, being not at any time either instructed by you or any other of my said honourable lords, how to use my said nieces; considering that I have, in some cases, thought good that my said nieces should not all wholly be their own guides, but rather willing them to follow mine advice, which they have not taken in such good part as my good meaning was, nor according to my expectation in them."[65]

Anne Seymour reclaimed the custody of her children in 1553.

NOTES

[1] *Calendar of State Papers, Spain,* Volume 9: 15 September 1549.
[2] Derek Wilson, *In the Lion's Court*, p. 499.
[3] *Calendar of State Papers, Spain,* Volume 9, 1547-1549, 8 October 1549.
[4] The following description of events is based on three accounts: A. J. A. Malkiewicz's "An Eye-Witness's Account of the Coup d'État of October 1549" in *The English Historical Review*, Vol. 70, No. 277 (Oct., 1955), pp. 600-609; letter from Ambassador Van Der Delft to Charles V, 8 October 1549, in *Calendar of State Papers, Spain*, Volume 9, 1547-1549; and *Acts of the Privy Council of England*, Volume 2, 1547-1550, pp. 330-340.
[5] Walter Raleigh, *The Works of Sir Walter Ralegh*, p. 175.
[6] BL Add MS 48126, ff. 2-5b.
[7] *Calendar of State Papers, Spain,* Volume 9, 1547-1549, 13 August 1549.
[8] *The Letters of William, Lord Paget of Beaudesert, 1547-63,* p. 33.
[9] John Gough Nichols, *Literary Remains of King Edward the Sixth*, Volume 2, p. Cxx.
[10] Nicholas Pocock (ed.), *Troubles Connected with the Prayer Book of 1549*, Camden Society, p. 121.
[11] The title originally belonged to John's mother, Elizabeth Grey, who was *suo jure* Viscountess Lisle. When she died c. 1525, she was married to Arthur Plantagenet, who retained the title. His second

wife, Honor, was then known as Lady Lisle. Arthur was arrested and died in the Tower in 1542.

12 *Calendar of State Papers, Spain,* Volume 9, 1547-1549, entry for 10 February 1547.

13 Modern writers, however, emphasize that such reports were aimed at slandering John Dudley's reputation after he himself was executed in 1553. Christine Hartweg, *Was John Dudley Behind the Death of Thomas Seymour?* www.allthingsrobertdudley.wordpress.com/2012/05/29/was-john-dudley-behind-the-death-of-thomas-seymour/

14 TNA PROB 11/37/342: The last will of Jane Dudley, Duchess of Northumberland.

15 D. M. Loades, *John Dudley, Duke of Northumberland, 1504-1553*, p. 104.

16 John Edward Jackson, *Wulfhall and the Seymours*, p. 13. Marjorie Blatcher (ed.), *The Seymour Papers 1532-1686*, p. 341.

17 *Letters of Richard Scudamore to Sir Philip Hoby*, Volume 39 of Camden Fourth Series, p. 104.

18 *Calendar of State Papers, Spain,* Volume 9: 19 December 1549.

19 The *Cronica del Rey Enrico Ottavo da Inglaterra* is attributed to Antonio de Guaras, a Spanish merchant who lived in London. It is often known as the *Spanish Chronicle* and was edited by M.A.S. Hume in 1889.

20 M.A.S. Sharp Hume, *Chronicle of King Henry VIII*, pp. 190-192.

21 *Letters of Richard Scudamore to Sir Philip Hoby*, Volume 39 of Camden Fourth Series, pp. 104.

22 *Calendar of State Papers, Spain,* Volume 10: 18 January 1549.

23 *Letters of Richard Scudamore to Sir Philip Hoby*, Volume 39 of Camden Fourth Series, pp. 112, 116.

24 *Calendar of State Papers, Spain,* Volume 10: 6 February 1550.

25 *Letters of Richard Scudamore to Sir Philip Hoby*, Volume 39 of Camden Fourth Series, p. 118.

26 *Calendar of State Papers, Spain,* Volume 10: 6 June 1550.

27 Ibid., 17 June 1550.

28 Ibid., 9 April 1551, 12 May 1551.

29 Ibid., 18 October 1551.

30 Ibid., 10 December 1551.

31 Chris Skidmore, *Edward VI*, Kindle edition.

32 *Calendar of State Papers, Spain,* Volume 10, 26 October 1551.

33 Ibid.

---

[34] Hastings Robinson, *Original Letters Relative to the English Reformation*, Volume 1, p. 342.
[35] John Gough Nichols, *Literary Remains of King Edward the Sixth*, Volume 2, p. 355.
[36] Ibid., p. 361.
[37] *Calendar of State Papers, Spain,* Volume 10, 10 December 1551.
[38] Ibid.
[39] Ibid.
[40] John Gough Nichols, *Literary Remains of King Edward the Sixth*, Volume 2, p. 374.
[41] Ibid.
[42] *Calendar of State Papers, Spain,* Volume 10, 1550-1552, 10 December 1551.
[43] John Gough Nichols, *Literary Remains of King Edward the Sixth*, Volume 2, p. 374.
[44] *Acts of the Privy Council of England*, Volume 3, p. 391.
[45] Henry Ellis, *Original Letters, Illustrative of English History*, Volume 2, p. 215.
[46] John Gough Nichols, *Literary Remains of King Edward the Sixth*, Volume 2, p. 384.
[47] Richard Grafton, *Grafton's Chronicle*, p. 529.
[48] Ibid., pp. 527-529.
[49] *Calendar of State Papers, Spain,* Volume 10, 1550-1552, 12 February 1552.
[50] Ibid.
[51] John Gough Nichols, *Literary Remains of King Edward the Sixth*, Volume 2, p. 390.
[52] *Calendar of State Papers, Spain,* Volume 10, 1550-1552, 12 February 1552.
[53] Sir John Hayward, *The Life and Raigne of King Edward the Sixth,* p. 147.
[54] John Gough Nichols, "Anne Duchess of Somerset", *The Gentleman's Magazine 23 (1845)*, p. 372.
[55] Sir John Hayward, *The Life and Raigne of King Edward the Sixth,* p. 131.
[56] Ibid., p. 133.
[57] *Acts of the Privy Council of England*, Volume 3, p. 466.
[58] *Calendar of State Papers, Spain,* Volume 10, 1550-1552, 12 February 1552.
[59] John Gough Nichols, "Anne, Duchess of Somerset", *Gentleman's Magazine*, April 1845, p. 373.

---

[60] *Acts of the Privy Council of England*, Volume 3, 1550-1552, p. 483.
[61] Ibid., p. 495.
[62] *Calendar of State Papers, Spain,* Volume 10, 1550-1552, 12 February 1552.
[63] Wilbur Kitchener Jordan, *Edward VI: Treshold of Power*, p. 337.
[64] Hastings Robinson, *Original Letters Relative to the English Reformation*, Volume 1, p. 342.
[65] Mary Anne Everett Wood, *Letters of Royal and Illustrious Ladies of Great Britain*, p. 260-62.

CHAPTER 7: THE DUDLEYS ASCENDANT

With the Duke of Somerset dead, Northumberland asserted his dominance at court. In January 1552, the imperial ambassador remarked how during an audience the King "kept his eye turned towards the Duke" and later "got up to withdraw because of signs the Duke of Northumberland made to him".[1] Just as Somerset put his trusted men about Edward VI, Northumberland installed his own creatures about the King. Northumberland's "intimate friend" John Gates became a member of the Privy Chamber and was said to have been "the principal instrument which he used in order to induce the King to something when he did not want it to be known that it had proceeded from himself". "All of the others who were in the [Privy] Chamber were creatures of the Duke", according to a French observer.[2] All contemporary commentators remarked on how influential Northumberland was with the King. "The Duke had given the young King such an opinion of himself that he treated him as if he were his subject", wrote the French ambassador and described how Northumberland exerted his influence:

"Whenever there was something of importance that he wanted done or spoken by the King without anyone knowing that it came from him, he would come secretly at night into the prince's chamber after everyone was abed, unnoticed by anyone. The next morning this young prince would come to his Council and, as if they came from himself, advocate certain matters—at which everyone marvelled, thinking they were his own ideas."[3]

Yet Edward VI was far from Northumberland's puppet. "I carefully observed the King's face and manners", reported the watchful imperial ambassador Jehan Scheyfve, "and he seems to be a likely lad of quick, ready and well-developed mind; remarkably so for his age". "For this very reason he runs great dangers", Scheyfve wrote to Charles V, adding that "if he were well and conscientiously instructed he would become a very noteworthy prince". Northumberland, whom the young King "seems to love and fear, is beginning to grant him a great deal of freedom in order to dispel the hostility felt for him, and to cause the King to forget the Duke of Somerset as quickly as possible".[4]

Yet Edward was not afraid to voice his own opinions. He once snapped at Northumberland whilst out at archery practice, saying that he had "aimed better when you cut off the head of my uncle Somerset".[5] He was emerging as a King who was to be both feared and loved, just as Henry VIII had been.

Northumberland was becoming ever more unpopular with the foreign ambassadors, who spread various rumours about him. In November 1550, the imperial ambassador reported that he heard "from a safe source" that he was "about to cast off his wife and marry my Lady Elizabeth, daughter of the late King, with whom he is said to have had several secret and intimate personal communications; and by these means he will aspire to the crown".[6] This "safe source" may have been Lady Mary, who was the imperial ambassador's chief informant and bore small love for both Northumberland (whom she once dubbed "the most unstable man in England") and her half sister, whom she firmly believed was the product of Anne Boleyn's extramarital affair with one of her lovers.[7] In fact, Northumberland and his wife were very close and it is unlikely that he had ever contemplated discarding her. Later in her life Jane Dudley said that her husband "was to me and to my mind the best gentleman that ever a living woman was matched withal", a powerful statement from a woman whose marriage was, as most Tudor marriages, arranged.[8]

The couple had thirteen children together although some of them didn't reach maturity. Their eldest son Henry died in 1544 at the siege of Boulogne, aged nineteen. Thomas, their second son, died as a two-year-old. John, the third son, inherited his father's earldom of Warwick when John the elder was made Duke of Northumberland in 1551 and started carving his own career under his father's watchful eye. Ambrose, Robert, Guildford and Henry outlived their father. Charles, the eighth son, died at the age of eighth. John and Jane also had five daughters, but only two of them, Mary and Katherine, survived the perils of infancy and early childhood and lived to reach adulthood.

A touching letter written by Northumberland after his four-year-old daughter Margaret died still survives, shedding some light on the man's character. Writing to William Cecil on 3 June 1552, Northumberland explained the child's demise in great detail, hardly containing his grief:

"I have thought good to signify unto you what moveth me to suspect infection in the disease whereof my daughter died. First, the night before she died, she was as merry as any child could be, and sickened about three in the morning, and was in a sweat, and within a while after she had a desire to the stool; and the indiscreet woman that attended upon her let her rise, and after that, she fell to swooning, and then, with such things as they ministered to her, brought her again to remembrance, and so she seemed for a time to be meetly well revived, and so continued till it was noon, and still in a great sweating; and about twelve of the clock she began to alter again, and so in continual pangs and fits till six of the clock, at what time she left this life. And this morning she was looked upon, and between the shoulders it was very black, and also upon the one side of her cheek; which thing, with the suddenty, and also [that] she could brook nothing that was ministered to her from the beginning, moveth me to think that either it must be the sweat or worse, for she had the measles a month or five weeks before, and very well recovered, but a certain hoarseness and a cough remained with her still. This [is] as much as I am able to express, and even thus it was: wherefore I think it not my duty to presume to make my repair to his Majesty's presence till further be seen what may ensue of it."[9]

Surviving evidence highlights the fact that Northumberland and his wife deeply cared for their brood. In 1552, they wrote a joint letter to their son John, Earl of Warwick, gently chastising him for not approaching them about money. The young Warwick, married to Anne

Seymour the younger, had no substantial income of his own but for some reason hesitated to ask his parents for financial help. Full of understanding, Northumberland wrote:

"I had thought you had had more discretion than to hurt yourself through fantasies or care, especially for such things as may be remedied and holpen. Well enough you must understand that I know you cannot live under great charges. And therefore you should not hide from me your debts whatsoever it be for I would be loath but you should keep your credit with all men. And therefore send me word in any wise of the whole sum of your debts, for I and your mother will see them forthwith paid and whatsoever you do spend in the honest service of our master and for his honor, so you do not let wild and wanton men consume it, as I have been served in my days, you must think all is spent as it should be, and all that I have must be yours, and that you spend before, you may with God's grace help it hereafter by good and faithful service wherein I trust you will never be found slack, and then you may be sure you cannot lack serving such a master as you have towards whom the living God preserve, and restore you to perfect health and so with my blessing I commit you to his tuition."

The letter was signed: "Your loving Father. Northumberland." Jane added a postscript in her own hand: "Your loving mother that wishes you health daily Jane Northumberland."[10] There is also evidence that John and Jane cared about their children's personal happiness. The young Warwick married for a political alliance with the Seymours, and the way he felt about his wife remains unclear, although Thomas Norton, secretary to the Duke of Somerset, recorded that after her father's execution Anne Seymour the younger was "happily and honorably settled".[11]

Robert, who would later become the Earl of Leicester and a great favorite of Queen Elizabeth, had more luck and married for love on 4 June 1550. His bride, Amy Robsart, daughter of a country gentleman, was seventeen, similar age to Robert's. According to William Cecil's later statement, this was a "carnal marriage" that started with happiness but ended in woe.[12] The King was a guest of honor during the wedding and enthusiastically recorded it in his diary:

"Sir Robert Dudley, third son of the Earl of Warwick, married Sir John Robsart's daughter, after which marriage there were certain gentlemen that did strive who should first take a goose's head, which was hanged alive on two cross posts."[13]

Perhaps envious of her brother's love match, Mary Dudley decided to choose her own husband. She married Henry Sidney, Edward VI's intimate friend and companion, on 29 March 1551. It was a clandestine ceremony, kept secret from her parents. John and Jane apparently later approved of Mary's choice, and the young couple underwent another, this time public, wedding ceremony at the Dudley London house, Ely Place, on 17 May. Henry Sidney would later say that Mary was "a full fair lady, in mine eye, at least, the fairest".[14]

As the wife of the most influential politician of Edward VI's court, Jane Dudley's household didn't lack luxuries. She wore magnificently wrought gowns and adorned herself with splendid jewellery, but she didn't neglect intellectual pursuits. The Dudleys were fascinated with geography and astronomy. Jane commissioned two tracts from the noted polymath John Dee, who resided in her household. The family also owned clocks, maps and astrolabes. The Dudleys were a great Renaissance family, favored by their King.

NOTES

[1] *Calendar of State Papers, Spain,* Volume 10, 1550-1552, 14 January 1552.
[2] Derek Wilson, *The Uncrowned Kings of England: The Black Legend of the Dudleys*, p. 233.
[3] Jennifer Loach, *Edward VI*, p. 96.
[4] *Calendar of State Papers, Spain,* Volume 10, 1550-1552, 14 January 1552.
[5] Chris Skidmore, *Edward VI: The Lost King of England*, p. 301.
[6] *Calendar of State Papers, Spain,* Volume 10, 1550-1552, 4 January 1550.
[7] Henry Clifford, *The Life of Jane Dormer, Duchess of Feria*, p. 80.
[8] Read more in Chapter 8.
[9] P. F. Tytler, *England Under the Reigns of Edward VI and Mary, Volume 2*, pp. 115-116.
[10] *Historical Manuscript Commission, Pepys Manuscripts*, pp. 1-2.
[11] Hastings Robinson, *Original Letters Relative to the English Reformation*, Volume 1, p. 342.
[12] Ewan Butler, *The Cecils*, p. 55.
[13] John Gough Nichols, *Literary Remains of King Edward the Sixth*, Volume 2, p. 273-275.
[14] *Calendar of the Carew Manuscripts*, ed. Brewer, Bullen, p. 9.

CHAPTER 8: REVERSAL OF FORTUNE

The arrests of the Duke and Duchess of Somerset created a power vacuum at the court of Edward VI. With the influential Anne Seymour gone from the scene, her place was quickly taken by William Parr's wife. Elisabeth, Marchioness of Northampton, long waited for her moment to shine and finally debuted in her role as the primary hostess at court in the autumn of 1551. In November of that year, Marie de Guise, Dowager Queen of Scotland, landed in England on her way from France, where she visited her daughter, Mary Queen of Scots, betrothed to the French Dauphin. She originally planned to stop in at Rye, but the autumn storms made it impossible, and the Dowager Queen "took landing by force of weather" at Portsmouth.[1] The imperial ambassador reported to Charles V:

"It is believed that the Queen Dowager of Scotland has arrived at Portsmouth to avoid your Majesty's ships, and that she will pass through London and visit the King, after which she will go on towards Scotland without delay. The Marquis of Northampton has been chosen to go to meet and welcome her."[2]

William Parr had been chosen to welcome her because he had recently returned from a successful embassy to France where he invested Henri II with the Order of the Garter as part of an ambitious plan, eagerly promoted by John Dudley, to marry the French King's daughter Elisabeth de Valois to Edward VI. That October, the Privy Council issued:

"Letters to divers noblemen and ladies to attend upon the Lord Marquis of Northampton and the Lady Marchioness, his wife, for receiving of the Queen Dowager of Scotland at Hampton Court."[3]

At first, Edward VI planned that the honour of entertaining Marie de Guise at Hampton Court would belong to his half sister Mary, who, as next in line to the throne, was the most important woman in the country. Yet Mary feared that the King might detain her at court or worse, "talk to her about the new religion and urge her to adopt it" and politely declined the offer, citing her notoriously ill health.[4]

Marie de Guise landed at Portsmouth on 22 October, and the King immediately sent a delegation to welcome her on English soil and outline her progress to London. On her way towards the capital, she lodged at the estates of various nobles. On 30 October, she reached Guildford, where she was welcomed by Sir William Howard and the nobility and gentry of Surrey. She was then solemnly conducted towards Hampton Court. About a mile from the palace, she was welcomed by William Parr, with 120 other gentlemen, and escorted to the gates. Edward VI recorded Marie de Guise's arrival in his *Chronicle*:

"At the gate thereof met her the lady Marchioness of Northampton, the Countess of Pembroke [Anne Herbert], and divers other ladies and gentlewomen to the number of three scores [sixty], and so she was brought to her lodgings on the Queen's side, which was all hanged with arras, and so was the hall, and all the other lodgings of mine in the house, very finely dressed. And for this night and the next day all was spent in dancing and pastime, as though it were a court and great presence of gentlemen resorted thither."[5]

The Queen stayed at the palace until 2 November. The next day she was escorted by a royal barge to the Bishop of London's residence, where she lodged overnight and was visited by a delegation of lords and ladies in the morning, including the Duchess of Northumberland and her daughter. On 4 November, the Queen was solemnly escorted to the Palace of Westminster, accompanied by the cream of the English womenfolk. On that day, the King's first cousins, Margaret Douglas and Frances Grey, opened the procession, followed by the Duchesses of Richmond and Northumberland, Lady Jane Grey (daughter of Frances), the Marchionesses of Northampton and Winchester, and the Countesses of Arundel, Bedford, Huntingdon and Rutland, with "hundred other ladies and gentlewomen". At the palace's gate, she was received by the Duke of Northumberland and the Earl of Pembroke "with all the sewers and carvers, and cupbearers, to the number of thirty".[6] Inside, Marie de Guise finally met the King, who "received her in most honorable and gracious fashion, coming forward to greet her halfway down the hall".[7] A splendid banquet followed, with the Queen dining under the same cloth of estate as the King, sitting on his left side. During one of the courses, she sat at a high table with Margaret Douglas and Frances Grey. Scholar John Aylmer scoffed at the ladies of the court who had their hair "frounced, curled and double-curled" and were "dressed and painted like peacocks".[8]

Marie de Guise's visit to England was one of the rare opportunities for women to become a visible presence at court. It reminded many of the past, when they were able to pursue careers as ladies-in-waiting to Henry VIII's wives. With no Queen to serve, noblewomen contended with running their own vast households. They also had more time to pursue their studies; the Edwardian period produced a number of female scholars. In 1551, Elisabeth Parr ordered a translation of the third book of Baldassare Castiglione's *Il Libro del Cortegiano* into English. Sir Thomas Hoby, translator and diplomat who entered William Parr's service in the 1550s, later recalled that he started translating this Renaissance text after he left for Paris:

"After I had conveyed my stuff to Paris and settled myself there, the first thing I did was to translate into English the third book of the 'Cowrtisan', which my Lady Marquess had often willed me to do, and for lack of time ever deferred it."[9]

The text, divided into four books, was printed in 1561 under the title *Il Cortegiano, The Courtyer of Count Baldessar Castilio.* At the head of the printed edition stands a note which records that the book was "Englisshed at the request of the Ladye Marquesse of Northampton, in anno 1551". Elisabeth's choice of Book III is highly significant, as it "entreateth of a Gentlewoman of the Courte". Historians argue that by commissioning the text, Elisabeth "both marked and assisted her newfound legitimacy in the courtly circles of Edwardian England".[10] In 1551, her marriage to William Parr was finally recognized by an Act of Parliament proclaiming that the Marquis of Northampton, "being separate, divorced, and at liberty, by the laws of God, to marry . . . solemnly and lawfully did marry the good and virtuous Lady Elisabeth".[11] Elisabeth's commission of the book celebrated her official recognition as William's wife.

By February 1553, Elisabeth was so influential at court that she was invited to take a prominent part during Lady Mary's entry to London. Mary was accompanied through the streets of the capital by "a great number of lords and knights, and all the great ladies". Elisabeth Parr was among them, as were the Duchesses of Northumberland and Suffolk.[12] The King's sister was received with great honors, "as if she had been Queen of England". She was received in Edward VI's bedchamber since he was ill and confined to bed. Edward entertained Mary with "small talk", carefully avoiding the subject of religion that had divided them during the previous years.[13] The visit underlined Mary's importance as Edward's successor.

Elisabeth Parr formed close friendships with Jane Dudley, Duchess of Northumberland, and Frances Grey, Duchess of Suffolk. In fact, Elisabeth was the one who suggested a marriage alliance between Jane's son Guildford and Frances's daughter Jane. In retrospect, the match was significant since Lady Jane Grey became Edward VI's successor in the summer of 1553. John Dudley was blamed for aiming for the crown by marrying his son to the Lady Jane, but it appears that he wasn't the one who insisted on the match and originally planned to match Guildford with Lady Margaret Clifford. Roger Alford, servant of Sir William Cecil, recorded:

"I remember you first opened the matter to me covertly in Greenwich Park, by asking of me, what was reported of the marriage of the Lord Guildford to the Lady Jane, the Duke of Suffolk's daughter; wherein you said, that the Lady Marquess of Northampton was then the greatest doer."[14]

That she was the original matchmaker is further confirmed by a warrant of delivery of the "wedding apparel" to Jane Dudley, Frances Grey and Elisabeth Parr. Interestingly, those "certain parcels of tissue and cloths of gold and silver" previously belonged to the Duke and Duchess of Somerset.[15] The Dudley-Grey match that took place in May 1553 was to become one of the most important of Edward VI's reign and one that would lead the young couple and their families straight into the political turmoil following the King's death in the summer of that year.

The wedding of Jane Dudley's son Guildford to Frances Grey's daughter Jane was the social event of the year. It was to be a triple wedding that would far outshine the celebrations held for the Dudley-Seymour nuptials three years previously. The married couples were Guildford Dudley and Jane Grey, Henry Herbert and Katherine Grey, and Henry Hastings and Katherine Dudley. The weddings were celebrated at Durham House, the Dudleys' lavish London residence on the Strand that previously briefly belonged to Anne Boleyn's father. Edward VI was unable to attend since he was already descending into his final illness, but he gave his blessing to the three matches, sending gifts of clothing and jewellery to the couples.

Jane Dudley, Duchess of Northumberland, already knew that the King had certain plans touching the future of her teenaged son Guildford and his bride. Lady Jane Grey, born in May 1537 and named after Queen Jane Seymour, was the eldest daughter of Henry Grey, Duke of Suffolk, and his wife, Frances. The Greys had close ties to the royal family: Frances was the eldest daughter of Mary Tudor, Henry VIII's younger sister, and Charles Brandon, Duke of

Suffolk. In 1533, Frances married her father's ward, Henry Grey, Marquis of Dorset, the great-grandson of Elizabeth Woodville and her first husband, John Grey of Groby. In 1551, Henry Grey was created Duke of Suffolk after the male line of the Brandon Dukes of Suffolk became extinct.

Frances and Henry had three daughters: Jane, Katherine and Mary. Jane, the eldest, was their pride and joy. She was raised in the teachings of the New Religion and was more pious than her young age merited. She was also exceptionally talented and preferred reading Greek philosophers to hunting, as her tutor Roger Ascham later recorded in his memoirs. Ascham believed that Jane was naturally inclined to read great classical philosophers because she derived her birth "both on your father's side and on your mother's from kings and queens".[16] She had crowned kings and queens for her ancestors and was thus an illustrious match for Guildford Dudley. Some people even thought she was too great a match for the Duke of Northumberland's son.

The marriage was interpreted in the light of Edward VI's recent illness. In late April 1553, the imperial ambassador Jehan Scheyfve observed that the sixteen-year-old King was "undoubtedly becoming weaker as time passes". "The matter he ejects from his mouth is sometimes coloured a greenish yellow and black, sometimes pink, like the colour of blood", Scheyfve reported and added that the King's physicians were perplexed and did not know what to make of his symptoms. The ambassador also suspected that John Dudley had royal aspirations by matching his son with Lady Jane Grey, "whose mother is the third heiress to the crown by the testamentary dispositions of the late King [Henry VIII], and has no heirs male".[17]

By 1553, Frances had three daughters but no sons. According to Henry VIII's last will and testament dating to 1546, Frances's children were to inherit the throne if his own children—Edward, Mary and Elizabeth—were to die childless. Frances herself was not named as heiress to the throne in Henry's last will, but her children, regardless of whether they were male or female, were. In January 1547, when Henry VIII's son Edward VI succeeded, Frances's elder daughter, Jane, was effectively third in line to the throne, following Edward's illegitimate half sisters Mary and Elizabeth.

In the spring of 1553, as it dawned on him that he was dying, Edward VI drew up his "devise for the succession", a document that would change the lives of the Dudleys and Greys forever. "For the lack of issue male of my body", the frail King bequeathed his kingdom "to the issue male coming of the issue female, as I have after declared. To the Lady Frances's heirs males, if she have any; for lack of such issue before my death, to the Lady Jane's heirs males; to the Lady Katherine's heirs males; to the Lady Mary's heirs males; to the heirs males of the daughters which she [Frances Grey] shall have hereafter . . ." The devise also specified that if these women failed to produce male heirs, the crown was to pass on to the male offspring of Margaret Clifford, Frances's niece.

The early draft of the King's devise makes it clear that he did not originally plan to be succeeded by a female. It was only after he realised that he would die sooner than any male heir was born to his kinswomen that he decided to make a radical change to the document: "If I die without issue and there be none heir male", Edward reiterated once again, "then the Lady Frances to be Governess Regent . . . until some heir male be born, and then the mother of that child to be Governess." The situation envisaged by the dying King was politically dangerous, and he soon changed his devise for the last time. He was now convinced that Lady Jane Grey was eminently suitable to become his direct successor since she was of royal descent and Protestant faith. The phrase "Lady Jane's heirs males" was altered to

"Lady Jane *and her* heirs males".[18] With the addition of just two short words, Jane Grey became heiress to the throne.

With his "devise for the succession", Edward VI excluded his two half sisters from inheriting the throne. According to the terms of his father's 1544 Act of Succession, confirmed by Henry VIII's last will of 1546, Edward's elder half sister Mary stood to inherit the crown if he died without issue. Mary had grown up in the public eye and was a popular figure. Many assumed that she would soon become Queen, but Edward was horrified by the prospect of Mary inheriting his kingdom because he was afraid she would bring Catholicism back and undo all his religious reforms. "I am convinced that my sister Mary would provoke great disturbances after I have left this life", he told his councillors, adding that he planned to disinherit both Mary and Elizabeth. Edward reasoned that he had solid grounds to do so. As a woman of marriageable age, he feared Mary would "marry a foreigner and thus stir up trouble in the kingdom and introduce a foreign government".[19] Most of all, however, both of his half sisters had been declared Henry VIII's bastards, sufficient grounds to exclude them from succeeding. Following the precedent set in his father's last will, Edward VI also bypassed the heirs of Henry VIII's elder sister, Margaret Tudor, Queen of

Scots. This left the descendants of Edward's junior aunt, Mary the French Queen, and her husband, Charles Brandon, Duke of Suffolk.

The exclusion of his elder half sister, Mary, seemed rational since Edward always tried to convert her to Protestantism, and he was not personally attached to her. The exclusion of Elizabeth seemed suspicious to most people who knew how close the young King was to his "Sweet Sister Temperance", as he affectionately referred to her. The two often exchanged correspondence, and Elizabeth was a frequent guest at his court. Furthermore, she was of the same religious conviction as Edward. The exclusion of Elizabeth, as well as the fact that it was Lady Jane Grey and not her mother, Frances, who was named as the King's successor, brewed suspicions that Edward VI was pushed to designate his young cousin as his heiress to please John Dudley, who, by matching his son with the Lady Jane, "thus showed that the object of his ambition was to place the crown on the head of his son, husband to the Lady Jane".[20]

John Dudley's and his wife's behaviour seem to confirm this. Shortly after Lady Jane married her son, Jane Dudley promised her daughter-in-law that she would be allowed to reside with her mother, but when the duchess learned from her husband that Edward VI's health was rapidly deteriorating, she changed her mind. Lady Jane later recalled that the Duchess of Northumberland told her that "if God willed to call the King to his mercy, and there was at that time no hope of his life, it would be needful for me to go immediately to the Tower, since His Majesty had made me heir to his kingdom". Lady Jane was "greatly moved" since she had no idea that Edward VI had designated her as his heiress. This knowledge "disturbed my mind", she recalled, "and after some time it oppressed me still more". Lady Jane "gave little heed" to her mother-in-law's words and returned to her mother, Frances. Jane Dudley was "much displeased with me and with the duchess my mother, saying that if she had resolved to keep me in the house, she had also kept her son, with whom she thought I would assuredly have gone", Lady Jane recalled. She remained three days in the Dudley household but fell ill and was allowed to depart to Chelsea Place to recuperate. While Jane Grey was recovering from her malady, the King was dying. Royal physicians agreed that Edward VI was suffering from "a suppurating tumour on the lung", but the restoratives they applied did him no good. "He is beginning to break out in ulcers; he is vexed by a harsh, continuous cough, his body is dry and burning, his belly is swollen, he has a slow fever upon him that never leaves him", wrote the imperial ambassador Jehan Scheyfve.[21] In late June 1553, the ambassador had no illusions that the young King had more than a few days to live:

"I have this very instant been informed that the King of England's present condition is such that he cannot possibly live more than three days. It is firmly believed that he will die tomorrow, for he has not the strength to stir, and can hardly breathe. His body no longer performs its functions, his nails and hair are dropping off, and all his person is scabby."[22]

By 4 July 1553, it was well known at court that Edward VI had changed the succession and appointed Lady Jane Grey as his heiress. This caused a stir among the ambassadors and certain councillors, who blamed the Duke of Northumberland for this sudden change. In his desperate attempt to save the dying monarch, Northumberland appointed "a certain woman who professes to understand medicine" to prolong the King's life so that he could lay the foundation for the accession of Lady Jane and his son, but she too was unable to ease the King's pain. Soon rumours spread across the country that Northumberland was "a great tyrant" who had "poisoned the King" so that he could place his own son on the throne.[23]

When Edward VI—swollen, bald and covered in ulcerous bedsores—died on 6 July 1553, his death was kept secret from the public. Wasting no time, Jane Dudley sent her daughter Mary to fetch Jane Grey from Chelsea Manor to their estate at Syon.[24] When Lady Jane arrived, there was no one to greet her, but after some time she met with John Dudley, Duke of Northumberland, William Parr, Marquess of Northampton, and other leading members of the nobility who acknowledged her as their new sovereign lady, to Jane's "extreme confusion".

"After a time they brought to me the Duchess Frances my mother, the Duchess of Northumberland, and the Marchioness of Northampton", she recalled. Then, in the presence of these three women and other lords, John Dudley informed Jane officially that Edward VI had died and she was now Queen of England. To calm her down, Dudley also told her that the Ladies Mary and Elizabeth, the King's half sisters, were excluded from succession and had no right to claim their royal inheritance.

When the lords told Lady Jane that the late King urged them "to shed their own blood freely, and to offer their own lives to death in this cause", she listened with "extreme grief of mind". Then, overcome "by sudden and unlooked for sorrow", the girl "fell to the ground, weeping very bitterly". She was inadequate, she protested, and it grieved her to hear of the King's death. She accepted the dubious honour of becoming the first English Queen regnant with reluctance. "For although I took upon me that of which I was unworthy, yet no one can say that I ever sought to obtain it for myself, nor ever solaced myself therein, nor accepted it willingly", she later recalled.[25]

Lady Jane was conducted to the Tower of London on 10 July 1553, accompanied by "a great company of lords and nobles . . . and many ladies".[26] Astonished crowds observed as the diminutive teenager swathed in cloth of gold and royal ermine entered the fortress, but nobody greeted her with the customary "Long Live the Queen".[27] Later that day she was proclaimed Queen in London. When Lady Jane was presented with the glistening royal crown, she was bashful and refused to try it on. William Paulet, Marquis of Winchester, who presented Lady Jane with the royal jewels, told her that another crown would soon be made for her husband, who would be crowned with her. Lady Jane was further displeased when Guildford asked her "to be made king", and then it dawned on her that she was indeed only a puppet in the hands of John Dudley. Lady Jane refused to be bullied into submission and called the Earls of

Arundel and Pembroke, informing them that "if the crown belonged to me, I would be content to make my husband a duke, but I would never consent to make him king". Neither John Dudley nor his wife expected this turn of events. The Duchess of Northumberland was so displeased with her daughter-in-law that she found "occasion for much wrath and disdain". "She became very angry with me, and was so displeased, that she persuaded her son not to sleep with me any longer", Lady Jane recalled. Guildford obeyed his mother and left Jane's company, vowing that "he would not in any way be made a duke, but king".[28]

In the meantime, Lady Mary, Edward VI's thwarted half sister, made her bid for the throne. On 11 July 1553, she sent her messenger to the Tower to announce to Lady Jane and her Council that she expected them to yield to her authority and accept her as Queen. Hearing this, the Duchesses of Northumberland and Suffolk "began to lament and weep", but their men decided to seize Lady Mary, whom they branded as a rebel and bastard.[29] Lady Jane's father was chosen to lead an army against Lady Mary, but his daughter begged the Council to let him stay. Instead, the Duke of Northumberland was designated to lead the army in Lady Jane's name. "Well, since you think it good, I and mine will go, not doubting of your fidelity to the Queen's

Majesty, which I leave in your custody", Northumberland told those who stayed in the Tower.[30] This was the last time Jane Dudley saw her husband as a free man.

With Northumberland gone, Lady Jane's councillors began to worry. None of them expected Lady Mary to fight back, and many believed that she would have no army to fight with Northumberland's forces. Yet Lady Mary was a popular figure, especially in the northern parts of the country, where she had her seat since Henry VIII's reign, and many noblemen rallied to her cause. Without John Dudley's commanding presence in the Tower, Jane Grey's councillors began to crumble under pressure and deserted her. Dudley soon realized that Mary's popularity was too strong to mount an opposition, and he was captured as he marched to apprehend her.

Proclaimed Queen of England on 19 July 1553, Mary decided to punish those who opposed her, but her policy towards the rebels was rather lenient. She pardoned those councillors who bended their knee and accepted her reign but could not bring herself to forgive John Dudley and his family. The Queen perceived Lady Jane Grey as Dudley's puppet and announced that her conscience "would not permit her to have her put to death".[31] Lady Jane's mother was allowed to leave the Tower of London, but Jane Dudley,

Duchess of Northumberland, was detained in the Tower together with her hapless daughter-in-law and sons, where they reportedly received "sour treatment".[32] By 29 July, the duchess was released and decided to fight for the lives of her loved ones. One of the imperial ambassadors reported:

"The Duchess of Northumberland has been let out of prison sooner than was expected, and set out to meet the Queen to move her to compassion towards her children; but when she had arrived at a spot five miles from this place, the Queen ordered her to return to London, and refused to give her audience."[33]

Queen Mary was in no mood to forgive John Dudley, although she intended to pardon his sons. In her view, Dudley tried to cheat her out of her royal right, and this she could not forgive. Yet the Duchess of Northumberland hoped that the Queen, naturally inclined to be a merciful lady, would take pity on her beloved spouse. To achieve her goal, the duchess wrote a letter to Anne Paget, wife of the influential courtier William Paget. Paget had made a brilliant career under Henry VIII and Edward VI and swiftly transferred his allegiance to Queen Mary. He was instrumental in the reconciliation of a number of his colleagues to the Queen after what Mary perceived was

Northumberland's coup to put Jane Grey on the throne. Lady Paget immediately became the Queen's lady-in-waiting and had access not only to the Queen herself but, above all, to her favorites.

Jane Dudley's letter to Anne Paget is not only a testament to her perseverance and love for her family, but also proof that she knew who to flatter: "Now good Madam, for the love you bear to God, forget me not and make my Lady Marquess of Exeter my good lady to remember me to Mistress Clarencius, to continue as she had before for me. Good Madam, desire your lord as he may do in speaking for my husband's life: in a way of charity I crave him to do it." Gertrude Courtenay, Marchioness of Exeter, and Susan Clarencius were two of Queen Mary's closest friends and confidantes, and they did not shy away from exerting their influence. Jane Dudley hoped that they could intercede on her husband's behalf, but they were intelligent enough to grasp that the Queen wanted John Dudley dead. In her letter to Lady Paget, the Duchess of Northumberland went on to say that her family's troubles aggravated her health problems, and she had begun to "grow into weakness". The postscript she added to the letter is especially touching because it reveals the strength of her love for her husband:

"Good Madam, desire my lord to be good lord unto my poor five sons: nature can no otherwise do but sue for them, although I do not so much care for them as for their father who was to me and to my mind the best gentleman that ever a living woman was matched withal . . ."[34]

Yet her pleas for her husband's release were unsuccessful. On 18 August 1553, he was tried and sentenced to death. To the astonishment of those who knew him, Dudley converted to Catholicism, perhaps in the hope of Queen Mary sparing his life. Shortly before his death, Northumberland summoned the two eldest sons of the late Edward Seymour, Duke of Somerset. Tormented by guilt, he "asked their pardon for the injury he had done to their father, the Protector of England, and confessed that he had wrongly and falsely procured his death".[35]

Yet, the duke still clung to the hope that Queen Mary would forgive him. In a letter to the Earl of Arundel, Northumberland wrote that "a living dog is better than a dead lion" and begged Arundel to speak on his behalf with the Queen: "Oh, that it would please her good Grace to give me life! Yea, the life of a dog, if I might but live and kiss her feet, and spend both life and all in her honorable service."[36] Mary would not grant him "the life of a dog", and

Northumberland's execution went on as scheduled on 22 August 1553. Whether Gertrude Courtenay pleaded for his life remains uncertain, but Susan Clarencius apparently made an attempt to help. The imperial ambassadors reported that they did intercede, with much success, on behalf of William Parr, Marquis of Northampton, who was involved in Dudley's plot and "generally held to be one of the guiltiest after the Duke of Northumberland".[37] On 4 September 1553, the imperial ambassadors reported:

"We are informed that the execution of the sentences passed on the rest of the prisoners was delayed in the hope of obtaining a pardon; and that the Marchioness of Exeter, mother of Courtenay; Dame Clarentius and the said Marquis of Northampton's first wife [Anne Bourchier] have sued for his pardon."[38]

A rumor circulated at court that William Parr "may receive his pardon on condition that he shall take back his first wife and put away the daughter of Lord Cobham, whom he married as his second wife".[39] This was bad news for Elisabeth Parr, Marchioness of Northampton, whose life and reputation were now endangered. By the time Mary was proclaimed Queen in July, Elisabeth had returned from London to Winchester Palace where she and William had lived in luxury and opulence since 1547. However, when

Stephen Gardiner, Bishop of Winchester, was released from the Tower and invited by Queen Mary to become a member of her newly formed regime, Elisabeth lost her home. Late in July 1553, Gardiner "has sent word to the Marquis of Northampton's wife to quit the lodging given to the Marquis by the late King [Edward VI], which she has done".[40]

After her husband's execution, Jane Dudley, Duchess of Northumberland, was "stripped almost of all necessities of life" and had to rely on the Queen's charity.[41] On 4 September 1553, the imperial ambassadors reported that they heard rumors that Jane's sons were to be spared, and the duchess herself received "an income of 4,000 crowns, a furnished house and a pension of 300 crowns, besides (the enjoyment of) her own private possessions".[42] That was true since the inventory of John Dudley's goods carried out between 28 August and 13 September 1553 confirm this. The Queen graciously agreed that the Duchess of Northumberland should keep her entire wardrobe as well as gilt and silver plate. She was also allowed to retain the contents of her husband's bedchamber and "kitchen stuff".[43] After her husband's attainder, Jane lost their manor at Chelsea but successfully petitioned the Queen to have it returned to her. In early 1554, Queen Mary agreed and leased it to the duchess for life. In the winter of 1554, a rebellion aimed at preventing the Queen from marrying Philip of Spain was hatched by Thomas Wyatt and his co-conspirators. William Parr, who was released from the Tower in December 1553, was preventatively arrested again on 26 January 1554.[44] He was said to sympathize with the rebels, and he had good reasons to do so. In the autumn of 1553, Queen Mary officially proclaimed that the marriage between William and his beloved Elisabeth Brooke was invalid, and the marquis was ordered to take back his first wife, Anne Bourchier. Elisabeth lost her status as Marchioness of Northampton, and in the last will of her friend Jane Dudley, Duchess of Northumberland, she was referred to simply as "Elisabeth, daughter of the Lord Cobham".[45]

Whereas William was not personally involved in the rebellion, Elisabeth's brothers were intimately linked with the rebels. Thomas Wyatt the younger, after whom the rebellion was named, was Elisabeth's first cousin.[46] When he gathered men in his ancestral seat at Allington Castle in Kent, Elisabeth's brothers Thomas and George were present.[47] Elisabeth's father, George Brooke, 9th Baron Cobham, was also involved, although to what extent remains unknown. On 30 January 1554, Thomas Wyatt and his armed forces besieged Cooling Castle, the Cobham family seat. Baron Cobham later maintained that his sons helped him defend the castle, but rumors swirled at court that Wyatt attacked Cooling to conceal their secret alliance. Despite his later efforts to explain his actions to the Queen's Council, Baron Cobham was incarcerated in the Tower on 2 February 1554.[48] When, four days later, Wyatt and his army entered London, Elisabeth's brothers George the younger, William and Thomas were with him.[49] They were also thrown into the Tower.

As the rebellion's result, Queen Mary, urged by her advisors, signed the death warrants of Lady Jane Grey and Guildford Dudley. The pair was executed on 12 February 1554. Guildford went first. Protestant to the last, he refused to have a Catholic priest attend him on the scaffold and as a result had no "ghostly father", or confessor, with him. After a "small declaration", he knelt down and said his prayers. Then, after desiring the assembled to pray for him, he laid his head on the block. It took one stroke of the axe to end his life. William Parr, still incarcerated in the Tower, witnessed Guildford's execution.[50] Guildford's lifeless body was thrown onto a cart and wheeled into the Chapel of St Peter ad Vincula for burial. Lady Jane Grey, whose window overlooked the chapel's courtyard, saw his headless corpse before she went to her own execution, a "sight to her no less than death". In the last letter she penned to her father, Lady Jane admitted that she greeted the end of her "woeful days" with joy.[51] Yet at the scaffold, when she was blindfolded and could not find the wooden block she was supposed to lay her neck on, she panicked. "What shall I do? Where is it?" she cried out, terrified. A touched bystander gently guided her to the block, where she put her head and stretched out her arms. The axe fell on her delicate neck: "And so she ended."[52] She was only seventeen.

Elisabeth Brooke's father and brothers were released on 24 March 1554, except for Thomas, who was sentenced to be hanged. He eventually left the Tower walls as a free man, but his signature, "Thomas Cobham 1555", can still be seen inside the Beauchamp Tower.

Wyatt's Rebellion did not stop Queen Mary from marrying Charles V's son. The royal marriage was celebrated on 25 July 1554 at Winchester Cathedral, with the Queen and King Philip wearing matching gowns of cloth of gold, blazing with diamonds. The court submerged itself in lavish entertainments celebrating the Anglo-Spanish alliance, and Jane Dudley, who was officially pardoned on 2 May 1554, decided to seek help from the Spanish lords and their wives who had arrived in Prince Philip's entourage.[53]

Jane met with kindness and understanding from the Spaniards. Ambassador Don Diego Hurtado de Mendoza, who was her late son Guildford's godfather, continued to show her "great friendship" and introduced her to the Spanish nobles. The Duke of Salvan and other members of Philip's Privy Chamber "did her sons good" by interceding on their behalf with their royal master. Maria Enríquez de Toledo y Guzmán, Duchess of Alva, also showed her goodwill towards the Dudley boys. Jane implored her to continue to be "a good Lady to all her children, as she has begun".[54]

Jane Dudley's efforts bore fruit. Her eldest son John, Earl of Warwick, was released from the Tower but died several days later, on 21 October 1554, at Penshurst Place, where his sister Mary lived with her husband, Henry Sidney.[55] Robert, Ambrose and Henry were also released and in early 1555 took part in jousts celebrating the Anglo-Spanish amity organized by Prince Philip.

In her last will, Jane bequeathed numerous goods to the Spaniards who helped to secure their releases; the Duchess of Alva received a green parrot, and Don Diego Hurtado de Mendoza was the recipient of a "book clock".[56] Jane Dudley's last will proved that Queen Mary did show her mercy since Jane was able to retain some of her former lands, income and luxuries she had amassed as the Duke of Northumberland's wife. She was thus able to bequeath exquisite clothes to her daughters: Mary, Lady Sidney, received a gown of black velvet furred with sables and a high-necked gown of "fair wrought velvet" while Katherine, Lady Hastings, received "a gown of new purple velvet, a summer gown, and a kirtle of purple velvet to it" with matching sleeves. Jane also remembered her three daughters-in-law, bequeathing gowns of rich materials to them. Among other items bequeathed to her children, relatives and friends were beds, Turkish carpets, chairs, cushions, rings ("one of my black enameled rings" was willed to Lord Paget), exquisitely wrought hangings, saddles and clocks that she seemed to especially value.

Jane's interest in astronomy dated to the reign of Edward VI, when she ordered two tracts on geography and astronomy from John Dee, mathematician, astronomer and astrologer who was to become famous during the reign of Queen Elizabeth I. An interest in clocks and astronomy was apparently something she had in common with her late husband. Mary Sidney, who appears to have been Jane's favorite daughter, received a clock "she did so much set by, that was the Lord her Father's, praying her to keep it as a jewel". Jane also remembered women whom she considered her friends. Anne Paget, who was the recipient of Jane's beseeching letter in 1553, received a "high-backed gown of wrought velvet", whereas Susan Clarencius, who apparently also made an attempt to intercede with Queen Mary, received a "tawny velvet jewel coffer". Elisabeth Parr, who suggested a match between Guildford Dudley and Jane Grey, was still held in great esteem: she received a black gown furred with lynx and furniture from the Duchess of Northumberland's own bedchamber.[57]

The exact date of Jane Dudley's death remains unknown; according to the inscription on her tomb, she passed away on 22 January 1555. As she lay dying in her luxurious four-poster bed surrounded by the vestiges of her former glory, Jane contemplated the futility of spending her efforts building status and wealth for this life. In her last will, she requested a humble funeral for her "wretched carcass that hath had at times too much in this world, full of all vanities, defeats and guiles". She also cautioned that "whoever doth trust in this transitory world, as I did, may happen to have an overthrow, as I had".[58] Despite her wishes for a simple funeral, the duchess was buried with pomp on 1 February 1555. Chronicler Henry Machyn recorded:

"The first day of February was buried the Duchess of Northumberland, at Chelsea, where she lived, with a goodly hearse of wax and pencels and escutcheons, two banners of arms, and four banners of images with many mourners and with two heralds of arms. There was a majesty and the valence and six dozen of torches and two white branches, and all the church hanged in black and arms and a canopy borne over her to the church."[59]

Jane's tomb at Chelsea Old Church survives to this day, a fitting monument to a woman who fought for her sons' release from the Tower of London until her last breath. Perhaps an even better monument, enshrined in words, was written by Arthur Collins in the eighteenth century. Working with the original documents of the Dudley family at Penshurst Place, Collins asserted that "the Duchess of Northumberland was the greatest example of fortitude in mind in adversity and of modest virtue; and whose wisdom, care and prudence, restored her overthrown house, in a reign of cruelty and tyranny."[60]

NOTES

[1] Edgar Powell, *The Travels and Life of Sir Thomas Hoby*, p. 75.
[2] *Calendar of State Papers, Spain,* Volume 10, 1550-1552, 26 October 1551.
[3] *Acts of the Privy Council of England Volume 3, 1550-1552,* p. 397.

[4] *Calendar of State Papers, Spain*, Volume 10, 1550-1552, 31 October 1551.
[5] John Gough Nichols, *Literary Remains of King Edward the Sixth*, Volume 2, p. 359.
[6] Ibid., pp. 362-365.
[7] *Calendar of State Papers, Spain,* Volume 10, 1550-1552, 16 November 1551.
[8] John Strype, *Historical and Biographical Works*, Volume 13, p. 167.
[9] Edgar Powell, *The Travels and Life of Sir Thomas Hoby*, p. 75.
[10] Helen Smith, *"Grossly Material Things": Women and Book Production in Early Modern England*, p. 64.
[11] Stephen Gilmore, *Landmark Cases in Family Law*, p. 126.
[12] *The Diary of Henry Machyn*, p. 30.
[13] *Calendar of State Papers, Spain,* Volume 11, 1553, 17 February 1553.
[14] John Strype, *Annals of the Reformation*, p. 347.
[15] Eric Ives, *Lady Jane Grey: A Tudor Mystery*, p. 185.
[16] Roger Ascham, *The Whole Works of Roger Ascham*, Volume I, p. 239.
[17] *Calendar of State Papers, Spain,* Volume 11: 28 April 1553.
[18] *The Honourable Society of the Inner Temple*: Edward VI's "My devise for the succession", Inner Temple Library, Petyt MS 538.47, f. 317.
[19] *Calendar of State Papers, Spain,* Volume 11, 1553, entry for 10 July.
[20] Ibid., 24 July 1553.
[21] Ibid., 12 May 1553.
[22] Ibid., 24 June 1553.
[23] Ibid., 4 July 1553, 7 July 1553.
[24] The residence formerly belonged to the Duke and Duchess of Somerset.
[25] *Writings of Edward the Sixth, William Hugh, Queen Catherine Parr, Anne Askew, Lady Jane Grey, Hamilton, and Balnaves*, p. 29.
[26] *The Diary of Henry Machyn*, p. 35.
[27] *Calendar of State Papers, Spain,* Volume 11: 10 July 1553.
[28] *Writings of Edward the Sixth, William Hugh, Queen Catherine Parr, Anne Askew, Lady Jane Grey, Hamilton, and Balnaves*, p. 32.
[29] *Calendar of State Papers, Spain,* Volume 11: 11 July 1553.
[30] *The Chronicle of Queen Jane, and of Two Years of Queen Mary,* p. 5.
[31] *Calendar of State Papers, Spain,* Volume 11, 1553, entry for 16 August 1553.
[32] Ibid., entry for 22 July 1553.
[33] Ibid., entry for 29 July 1553.
[34] S. J. Gunn, "A Letter of Jane, Duchess of Northumberland, in 1553", *English Historical Review*, November 1999.

[35] *Calendar of State Papers, Spain*, Volume 11, 27 August 1553.
[36] D. M. Loades, *John Dudley, Duke of Northumberland, 1504-1553*, p. 269.
[37] *Calendar of State Papers, Spain*, Volume 11, 16 August 1553.
[38] Ibid., 4 September 1553.
[39] Ibid., 27 August 1553.
[40] Ibid., 27 July 1553.
[41] Arthur Collins, *Letters and Memorials of State*, p. 33.
[42] *Calendar of State Papers, Spain*, Volume 11, 1553, entry for 4 September 1553.
[43] D. M. Loades, *John Dudley, Duke of Northumberland, 1504-1553*, pp. 307-309.
[44] *Chronicle of Queen Jane*, p. 36.
[45] TNA PROB 11/37/342: The last will of Jane Dudley, Duchess of Northumberland.
[46] His mother was Elisabeth Wyatt, nee Brooke, sister of Elisabeth's father.
[47] David Loades, *Intrigue and Treason: The Tudor Court, 1547-1558*, p. 156.
[48] *Chronicle of Queen Jane*, p. 41.
[49] David Loades, *Intrigue and Treason: The Tudor Court, 1547-1558*, p. 92.
[50] *Chronicle of Queen Jane*, p. 55.
[51] Nicholas Harris Nicolas, *Memoirs and Literary Remains of Lady Jane Grey*, p. 47.
[52] *The Chronicle of Queen Jane*, p. 59.
[53] *Calendar of the Patent Rolls, Philip & Mary*, Volume 1, p. 418.
[54] TNA PROB 11/37/342: The last will of Jane Dudley, Duchess of Northumberland.
[55] *Henry Machyn's Diary*, p. 72.
[56] TNA PROB 11/37/342: The last will of Jane Dudley, Duchess of Northumberland.
[57] Ibid.
[58] Ibid.
[59] *Henry Machyn's Diary*, p. 81.
[60] Arthur Collins, *Letters and Memorials of State*, p. 3.

CHAPTER 9: IN AND OUT OF ROYAL FAVOUR

With no place for her among Queen Mary's conservative circle, Elisabeth Brooke lived away from court but kept in touch with her old friends. On 31 March 1555, she stood as one of the godmothers to a baby girl born to Elizabeth Cavendish, better known to history as Bess of Hardwick.[1] The second godmother was Katherine Grey, younger sister of the executed Lady Jane. Their association shows that there were no hard feeling between the Greys and Elisabeth Brooke, who was responsible for the marriage of Lady Jane and Guildford Dudley two years earlier.

In 1557, Elisabeth Brooke stepped out of the shadows and made her mark on politics. Elisabeth was never close with Mary Tudor, but she forged a strong friendship with the Queen's half sister, Lady Elizabeth. The two first met at court during the 1540s in the service of Katherine Parr; Elisabeth Brooke served as the Queen's maid of honour whereas Lady Elizabeth was listed as her "ordinary" attendant.[2] They continued to serve Katherine Parr in her dower household before Lady Elizabeth's departure to Cheshunt after the Seymour scandal. Queen Mary always detested Lady Elizabeth, who in her view "was born of an infamous woman".[3] Mary never forgave Anne Boleyn for what she perceived as breaking her family apart, and she saw Lady Elizabeth as a product of their father's adultery, nurturing painful memories of "the many injuries inflicted on her mother, the late Queen, and on herself" during the difficult 1530s.[4]

In 1554, Mary married Philip II of Spain, her Habsburg cousin, hoping that children born of this union would oust Lady Elizabeth from the succession. The Queen was heard saying that she would not allow her half sister to be her heiress "because of her heretical opinions, illegitimacy and characteristics in which she resembled her mother" and tried to get rid of Lady Elizabeth by any means possible.[5]

When Wyatt's Rebellion broke out shortly before the Queen's marriage took place, Mary was eager to find out whether her half sister was complicit. The evidence was damning since Wyatt acknowledged that he had sent Lady Elizabeth a letter, to which she replied verbally, sending her servant with a message that "she did thank him much for his goodwill and she would do as she should see cause".[6] The sole fact that Lady Elizabeth entered into communication with a traitor was damning enough. Simon Renard, the imperial ambassador Mary trusted, urged the Queen to send Elizabeth to the scaffold, but Mary refused, although she had briefly imprisoned her half sister in the Tower and later placed her under house arrest in the dilapidated palace of Woodstock.

In 1557, the Queen decided to force Lady Elizabeth to marry Emmanuel Philibert, Duke of Savoy. The plan was to take her to Flanders and marry her to the duke, even against her will. In this way, Queen Mary would not only get rid of her despised half sister, but also ensure her removal from England and, in the end, from royal succession. Yet the plan was met with hostility from the French, who hatched a plot to warn Lady Elizabeth of the danger she faced. French ambassador François de Noailles used Elisabeth Brooke as an intermediary, who warned Lady Elizabeth of the Queen's plans. Elizabeth was grateful and replied that "she would rather die than either of these things ever come to pass".[7] She would always remember Elisabeth's help.

Whereas Elisabeth Brooke led a quiet life away from court, Anne Seymour clawed her way back to the top. She was released from the Tower in August 1553 and quickly regained her wealth and status. Somerset House, her husband's lavish ducal palace, was given to Lady Elizabeth, who spent the night before Mary's coronation there, but Syon House was returned to Anne. In October 1553, she received part of her late husband's attainted goods, some of which had been retained by the executed Duke of Northumberland.[8] In November 1553, Anne was in London, writing to her "loving friend" John Thynne concerning certain lands and manors that belonged to her late husband since the Queen "hath resolved my son to be restored in blood only by Parliament, and meant to make him Earl of Hertford by creation, wherewith her Highness is bent to give him such lands as were my Lord's Grace at the death of King Henry". The Duke of Somerset was executed for felony, not high treason, and his death would not have affected his lands and estates. In theory, his eldest son was entitled to receive his titles and lands, but the Act of Parliament that passed shortly after Somerset's execution declared his estates forfeited to the crown. Therefore it required a new creation to make Somerset's son Earl of Hertford, and Anne enquired of John Thynne, her late husband's former steward, whether he had these lands and estates listed.[9]

Anne's friendship with the Queen that had started in the household of Katharine of Aragon blossomed, and Mary rewarded Anne for helping her in times past. Even their religious differences—Anne was still a Protestant whereas Mary staunchly held on to Catholicism—were not able to drive a wedge between them. In fact, the Queen even allowed her Archbishop of Canterbury, Reginald Pole, to give Anne license to eat meat during Lent, such was her religious tolerance for those she deeply cared for.[10] In 1556, the Queen gave Anne funds "towards reparation of Wolf Hall manor", the Seymour family seat, that was to pass to Anne's eldest son and heir, Edward, who was seventeen at the time.[11] Anne exchanged New Year's gifts with the Queen; in 1557, she gave Mary a smock "wrought all over" and received a gilt salt and jug weighting twenty-two ounces.[12] In 1558, the Queen granted Anne Hanworth Palace in Middlesex for life. It was a luxurious residence given by Henry VIII to Anne Boleyn in 1532 and later presented to Katherine Parr as her dower property. It was there that much of the scandal connected to Thomas Seymour and Lady Elizabeth had taken place in 1548, much to Anne's annoyance. Hanworth was a truly magnificent palace, a house where two queens had lived, and Anne made it her main residence for the rest of her life. For as long as Queen Mary lived, Anne Seymour's future was secured, but the accession of Mary's half sister Elizabeth in November 1558 meant a new era for the politically savvy

Duchess of Somerset. Would the daughter of Anne Boleyn prove bountiful to a Seymour?

NOTES

[1] Mary S. Lovell, *Bess Of Hardwick: First Lady of Chatsworth*, p. 92.
[2] *Letters and Papers, Henry VIII,* Volume 21 Part 1, note 969.
[3] *Calendar of State Papers, Venice,* Volume 6, n. 1274.
[4] *Calendar of State Papers, Spain,* Volume 5 Part 2, n. 48.
[5] *Calendar of State Papers, Spain,* Volume 11, entry for 28 November 1553.
[6] John Gough Nichols, *The Chronicle of Queen Jane and of Two Years of Queen Mary*, p. 56.
[7] Louis Wiesener, *The Youth of Queen Elizabeth 1533-1558*, Volume 2, p. 233.
[8] *Acts of the Privy Council of England,* Volume 4, 1552-1554, p. 355.
[9] John Edward Jackson, *Wulfhall and the Seymours*, p. 29.
[10] SE/VOL. IV/32, License from Reginald [Pole], Cardinal-Legate, to Anne, Duchess of Somerset, widow of the Protector, to eat meat in Lent except on Wednesday, Friday and Saturday; Lambeth.
[11] *Calendar of State Papers, Domestic Series, of the Reigns of Edward VI., Mary, Elizabeth, 1547-[1625]:* 1601-1603: Elizabeth; with addenda, 1547-1565, p. 448.
[12] David Loades, *Mary Tudor*, p. 359.

Chapter 10: In High Favour with the Queen

In the last year of Queen Mary's reign, Elisabeth Brooke lost her parents in the vicious influenza epidemic that swept through England in 1558. George, 9th Baron Cobham, passed away on 29 September, followed closely by his wife, who died on 1 November. William Brooke, the new Baron Cobham, erected a magnificent tomb in Cobham Church to the memory of his parents and added Latin verses celebrating their love: "Here Anne lies—a lady chaste and fair, Blest with her children's love and husband's care . . . 'Twas in the last sad year of Mary's reign that first the husband, then the wife, was ta'en."[1]

Elisabeth briefly lived with her parents after she lost her status in 1553, and it appears that she was close to both. The language their last wills are couched in implies that they still regarded Elisabeth as William Parr's wife despite Queen Mary's dissolution of the marriage. Baron Cobham listed her as "my daughter Elisabeth, lately called and known by the name of Lady Marquess of

Northampton".[2] Anne, Baroness Cobham, bequeathed to "my daughter, the Lady Marquess" her jewels and apparel, including a jewel set with diamonds with "a great pearl" pendant, three boxes of silver, two of her "best wrought handkerchiefs", a piece of gold "called a sovereign" and "the best ring I have".[3]

Sixteen days after the death of Elisabeth's mother, Queen Mary also succumbed to her final illness. Earlier in the year she had suffered another phantom pregnancy and was now severely depressed and mortally ill, possibly from an ovarian cyst, uterine cancer or influenza.[4] She died on 17 November 1558, aged forty-two, at St. James's Palace. Shortly before her death the Queen had appointed her half sister Lady Elizabeth as her successor.

Queen Elizabeth's accession changed Elisabeth Brooke's circumstances for the better. "I stood in danger of my life, my sister was so incensed against me", the Queen would reminisce later in her reign, no doubt feeling grateful to have had loyal friends who stood by her side during that dark period.[5] The new Queen was deeply grateful to Elisabeth Parr and amply rewarded her for her loyalty. In December 1558, when she went in procession from the Tower of London to Somerset House, Queen Elizabeth made a show of stopping by at the window of William Parr's house and talking to him for a long while, "asking him about his health in the most cordial way in the world". Parr, who was ill with quartan fever, could not participate in the procession but was apparently very devoted to the new Queen. The Spanish ambassador, Count Feria, wryly observed that "the only true reason for this was that he had been a great traitor to her sister, and he who was most prominent in this way is now best thought of".[6] In the immediate aftermath of Elizabeth's accession, William Parr was reinstated to his former dignity of Marquis of Northampton, and his marriage to Elisabeth Brooke was proclaimed valid again. Not only were Elisabeth and William the Queen's intimates, but Elisabeth's brothers were also her great favourites. In the end of November 1558, the Queen sent William Brooke, 10th Baron Cobham, as an ambassador to Philip of Spain in order to relay to him official information about Queen Mary's death. The Count of Feria, Philip's ambassador at the English court, wrote:

"The Queen decided three days ago to send Lord Cobham to your Majesty. He is the son of the Lord Cobham whom you knew and who recently died. They told me nothing about it until yesterday when Secretary Cecil sent to say that Cobham was going and had been ordered to visit me before he left. This he did last evening but the object of his going is only to inform your Majesty formally of what has occurred. He has no place in the Queen's household and he and his brother have not enjoyed a good reputation, but have always been adherents of the new Queen and she is attached to him. Your Majesty should have him well housed and treated, and a handsome chain or something should be given to him. I have written to my brother-in-law asking him to entertain him and to win his good graces."[7]

In February 1559, the ambassador included Elisabeth Parr in his despatch:

"Cobham has been, and is, so zealous with his letters from Brussels that it has been necessary to manage him a little, and his lordship has therefore thought well to promise him a pension, although he has not told him how much it will be. The Queen has promised him the wardenship of the Cinque Ports. The marchioness of Northampton, his sister, who is in high favour with the Queen, has served His Majesty when opportunity has occurred."[8]

Feria's despatch illustrates that within three months of Queen Elizabeth's accession Elisabeth Parr was a visible presence at court, and not only as a wife or sister of important men. Just what the ambassador meant when he wrote that Elisabeth "served" Philip when such an opportunity occurred remains unknown. Her high standing with the Queen was further emphasized by her political role at court.

Although Elizabeth Tudor is known to history as the Virgin Queen, in the beginning of her reign her councillors petitioned her to marry in order to establish the succession and avoid bloodshed in the future. Unlike her half sister Mary, Queen Elizabeth had no heir, and so the question of who would succeed her was very much on everyone's minds. When the first Parliament of Elizabeth's reign convened in the winter of 1559, her subjects formally petitioned the Queen to marry. Elizabeth responded with a statement on 10 February 1559, wherein she didn't refuse the prospect of marriage outright but didn't welcome it either. She put her future in God's hands and remarked: "And in the end this shall be for me sufficient, that a marble stone shall declare that a Queen, having reigned such a time, lived and died a virgin."[9]

Elizabeth manifested an aversion towards marriage early in her youth. Her childhood friend and the man who was appointed as Master of the Horse when she became Queen, Robert Dudley, later said that "they had first become friends before she was eight years old. Both then and later (when she was old enough to marry) she said she never wished to do so".[10] Nearly everyone in Elizabeth's immediate family had unpleasant experiences when it came to the institution of marriage. Her father married six times and beheaded two of his wives, including Elizabeth's mother. Her sister married Philip of Spain and fell in love with him, but it was a loveless match for Philip, who married Mary for political reasons. Finally, husbands—even when professing undying love towards their wives—could stray from the marital bed and seek out younger and more beautiful women, as evidenced by Thomas Seymour's romantic interest in the much younger Elizabeth back in 1548. It is even possible that Elizabeth abhorred the idea of marriage because she was afraid of bearing children; many women, including two of Elizabeth's stepmothers, perished as a result of childbed fever.

Early in her reign, Queen Elizabeth's hand in marriage was sought by various royals, including members of the Habsburg and Vasa dynasties. Some firmly believed that the Queen entered marriage negotiations in order to appease her subjects and take the heat off her relationship with Robert Dudley, son of the executed Duke of Northumberland. In April 1559, Count Feria remarked:

"During the last few days Lord Robert has come so much into favour that he does whatever he likes with affairs and it is even said that her Majesty visits him in his chamber day and night."[11] Yet Robert Dudley was a married man and the Queen's chief duty was to marry and produce heirs.

In the autumn of 1559, a delegation from Prince Erik of Sweden came to England. The Prince's brother, Duke John of Finland, acted as an ambassador who wooed the Queen in Erik's name. Queen Elizabeth's two chief favourites, Elisabeth Parr and Robert Dudley, were involved in the suit from its onset. On 5 October 1559, Duke John was welcomed in London by John de Vere, Earl of Oxford, and Robert Dudley. At Gracechurch Street, he was received by William Parr and Ambrose Dudley "and other gentlemen and ladies". On 27 October, the duke stood as one of the godfathers to Thomas Chamberlain's son. Chamberlain, a skilled diplomat and a rising start of the court, also chose Robert Dudley and Elisabeth Parr, a further indication that both were seen as highly regarded by the Queen.[12]

Elisabeth's status was in fact so high that the Queen ordered her to take part in the funeral of Frances Grey, Duchess of Suffolk, the Queen's first cousin and the marchioness's friend. Frances died on 21 November 1559, aged only forty-two, and was buried on 5 December at Westminster Abbey, where her tomb effigy can still be seen today. She was buried with honours due to her status as a member of the royal family. Her body was "brought and set under hearse, and the mourners placed, the chief at the head, and the rest on each side" while the King of Arms "with a loud voice" proclaimed:

"Laud and praise be given to Almighty God, that it hath pleased him to call out of this transitory life unto his eternal glory the most noble and excellent princess the Lady Frances, late Duchess of Suffolk, daughter to the right high and mighty prince Charles Brandon, Duke of Suffolk, and of the most noble and excellent Princess Mary, the French Queen, daughter to the most illustrious prince King Henry VII."[13]

Elisabeth's proximity to the Greys was evident at court, but it soon proved a dangerous connection. Frances's two remaining daughters, Katherine and Mary, were, according to Henry VIII's last will, heiresses to Queen Elizabeth's throne. Despite arranging a lavish funeral for their mother, however, the Queen harboured no warm feelings towards her children. Elizabeth was reluctant to name her successor, but the name of Katherine Grey was on everyone's lips since the Queen persistently refused to make a final decision about marriage.

Queen Elizabeth was known for her aversion towards marriage and childbearing, but her subjects still hoped that one day she would marry and settle the succession onto her own child. Only Elizabeth knew this was impossible since she believed herself incapable of bearing children. Foreign ambassadors often wrote about the Queen's intimate health, repeating rumours that "this woman is unhealthy, and it is believed certain that she will not have children".[14] Like her half sister, the Queen suffered from erratic menstrual periods caused by a hormonal imbalance. William Camden, the first biographer of Queen Elizabeth, who had access to many original documents, recorded the words of the Queen's private physician, Dr Robert Huicke, who believed Elizabeth would never marry because of her "womanish infirmity". As Queen, Elizabeth would marry to beget heirs rather than for love, and she was heard saying that "knowing herself incapable of children, she would never render herself subject to a man".[15]

Having no designated heir to succeed her, the Queen was pressured to name a successor. Early in her reign there were two possible candidates, both female. One of them was Elizabeth's cousin, Mary Stuart, Queen of Scots, who, like Elizabeth, ruled in her own right. The other was Elizabeth's English cousin Katherine Grey. Katherine, born in 1540, was favoured by most of the nobility in England, but the Queen hated her cousin so much that it was said that she "could not well abide the sight of her". Elizabeth knew well how dangerous it was to have a designated heir since she herself had been her half sister's successor for years. Many disgruntled nobles, unhappy with Queen Mary's regime, sought her approval and tried to manoeuvre her into backing their treasonous schemes. During Mary's reign, Elizabeth lived in fear of her own life since her name was always on the traitors' lips regardless of whether she backed them or not. It was the same with Lady Katherine Grey, who was courted by Elizabeth's political enemies, both at home and abroad. Henri II, King of France, was rumoured to be hatching plans to convey Katherine out of England and marry her to his own son or other noble in order to keep a pet claimant to the throne in his tight grip. Similar plans were discussed by the Spanish ambassador, who thought that Katherine could be "enticed away" to Spain and oppose Elizabeth from there. Katherine liked all the attention she received from foreign diplomats, and since the Queen failed to treat her appropriately to her rank, excluding her from the Privy Chamber, Katherine decided to strike back. On one occasion, she "had spoken very arrogant and unseemly words in the hearing of the Queen and others standing by".[16] She did not know that one day she would desperately need the Queen's approval.

Young and beautiful, Katherine fell in love with Edward Seymour, the eldest son of the Duchess of Somerset. Their romance started late in the reign of Queen Mary, when Katherine lived in the house of Anne Seymour at Hanworth. It was at Hanworth were Edward had first fallen in love with Katherine and broached the question of marriage. Lady Katherine became good friends with Edward's younger sister, Lady Jane Seymour, whom the young earl planned to use "for the only instrument or means to further his said purpose". Edward, the spitting image of his father, was handsome but also rash and volatile—"unruly" and "wilful", as his mother called him. Yet he wasn't as reckless as his mother believed, for when his secret marriage would later come to light, he sought to protect those who knew about it.

Katherine Grey later claimed that Edward "rode to the Lady Frances her mother to obtain her goodwill, who granted him the same and thereupon sent to the Court for the said Lady Katherine and moved her to grant her goodwill to the said Earl". Edward denied that he had ever sought Frances's approval for his match with her daughter, but he revealed that she treated him with great kindness and called him her "son", a sign that she approved of him as her daughter's prospective husband.

The examination of Adrian Stokes, Frances's husband, revealed that Edward lied since he "moved [pleaded with] her, the Lady Frances, to grant her goodwill that he might marry the Lady Katherine, her daughter". Indeed, Frances knew that her daughter was "very willing" to marry Edward, and she thought that he was "a very fit husband for her, if their marriage should please the Queen Elizabeth and her honourable Council".[17]

With the help of her husband, Frances drafted a letter to Queen Elizabeth trying to win her approval for the match: "The Earl of Hertford doth bear goodwill to my daughter the Lady Katherine, and I do humbly require the Queen's Highness to be a good and gracious lady unto her, and that it may please Her Majesty to assent to her marriage to the said earl." The marriage, Frances wrote, "was the only thing she desired before her death and should be the occasion for her to die the more quietly".[18]

Unfortunately for the young couple, the letter never reached Queen Elizabeth as Frances died before she could finish it.

Motherless, Katherine Grey was now effectively an orphan without parents to guide and protect her. After a period of mourning, Katherine decided to accept Hertford's proposal, and, together with his sister Jane, the brave trio made plans for a clandestine wedding ceremony. The couple married between 1 November and 25 December 1560. All three suspected that Queen Elizabeth would not consent to the match, and the girls lied to their sovereign to slip away from their courtly duties. Katherine said that she had a "swelling in her face" and could not accompany the Queen to Eltham for a hunting trip.[19] Jane offered to stay behind as well and take care of her friend. The next day, Katherine married Hertford at his house in Cannon Row, Westminster. Lady Jane, who acted as witness, found a priest to officiate the clandestine ceremony.

Katherine and Hertford consummated their union immediately after the wedding and continued their secret meetings over the coming months. They had sex in the maidens' chamber that Katherine shared with two other maids of honour at Greenwich and Windsor. Their "familiarity" was becoming ever more evident at court. William Cecil, Secretary of State, decided to separate the couple and arranged Hertford's departure to France, where the wayward earl would finish his education. Katherine already suspected she was with child, but, lacking knowledge about pregnancy, she couldn't confirm it before Hertford's departure in May 1561. Moved by compassion towards Katherine, Hertford gave her a deed that bequeathed her £1,000 of widow's jointure in case of his death abroad.

After Hertford's departure, Katherine continued to serve as the Queen's maid of honour. To her utter horror, she realized that her secret marriage was not such a secret after all. After a short conversation with William Cecil, Secretary of State, she had no illusions as to who had sent her husband abroad. Cecil "did advise her to take good heed how she proceeded in familiarity with the said Earl without making the Queen's Majesty privy thereunto". Cecil already knew that the couple were married.

Elisabeth Parr apparently knew as well, perhaps informed by Cecil, with whom she shared a close friendship since the late 1540s. Perhaps instructed by Cecil himself, Elisabeth took it upon herself to warn Katherine about the danger of continuing her relationship with Hertford behind the Queen's back. She was hoping that, as her late mother's friend, her warning would resonate with Katherine. Taking her good friend Lady Clinton with her as witness to the conversation, Elisabeth "did seriously advise her to beware the company and familiarity with the said Earl". But Katherine—young, naïve and madly in love with her "Ned", as she affectionately referred to Hertford in private—"denied, both unto Mr Secretary and others, that there was any such matter".[20]

It was too late for Katherine to conceal her marriage anyway since her pregnancy was becoming more visible. She managed to hide her growing belly beneath loose gowns for months, but by the summer of 1561 she was rapidly becoming a figure of scandal and subject of rumours at court. She was already in her seventh month and the baby was vigorously kicking in her belly when she wrote to Hertford, urging him to return. She received no reply. Finally, on 9 August 1561, Katherine decided to approach her mother's former servant, Bess Cavendish, the same woman to whose child she stood godmother, together with Elisabeth Parr, in 1555. Bess, now Lady St Loe, was another great favourite of the Queen's and Katherine hoped she might be able to help. She was bitterly disillusioned when Lady St Loe wept when she learned of Katherine's secret marriage and pregnancy, declaring she was "sorry . . . because she had not made the Queen's Majesty privy thereunto".

Desperate for allies, Katherine went to Robert Dudley's chamber in the middle of the night. Kneeling at his bedside, she sobbingly "required him to be a mean to the Queen's Highness for her". Unfortunately for Katherine, Dudley informed the Queen about her secret marriage and pregnancy, and the next day Elizabeth gave orders to conduct her cousin to the Tower of London. Katherine and Hertford suspected the Queen would be an obstacle to their marriage, but they both overlooked one important detail. As heiress to the throne, Lady Katherine's marriage was a matter of state, and, under the Royal Marriage Act of 1536, it was treason for anyone with royal blood to marry without the sovereign's consent. Katherine's pregnancy further irked the Queen, who decided to launch an investigation of her cousin's marriage.

NOTES

1 W. Scott Robinson, *Six Wills Relating to Cobham Hall*, pp. 199-304.
2 TNA PROB 11/43/628: Will of Sir George Brooke or Lord Cobham, of the Right Honorable Order of the Garter. Transcribed by Nina Green at http://www.oxford-shakespeare.com/Probate/PROB_11-43-628.pdf

---

[3] CP 198/110, the will of Anne, Lady Cobham, 7 October 1558. Transcribed by Nina Green at http://www.oxford-shakespeare.com/CecilPapers/CP_198-110.pdf

[4] *Calendar of State Papers, Spain,* Volume 13, 1554-1558, n. 498.

[5] Clark Hulse, *Elizabeth I: Ruler and Legend*, p. 26.

[6] *Calendar of State Papers, Spain (Simancas),* Volume 1, 1558-1567, 14 December 1558.

Wriothesley's Chronicle, Volume 2, p. 142.

[7] *Calendar of State Papers, Spain (Simancas),* Volume 1, 1558-1567, 25 November 1558.

[8] Ibid., 29 February 1559.

[9] Maria Perry, *The Word of a Prince*, p. 100.

[10] Simon Adams, *Leicester and the Court: Essays on Elizabethan Politics*, p. 139.

[11] *Calendar of State Papers, Spain (Simancas),* Volume 1, 1558-1567, n. 27.

[12] *The Diary of Henry Machyn*, p. 216.

[13] Ibid., p. 219.

[14] *Calendar of State Papers, Spain (Simancas),* Volume 1, 1558-1567, n. 122.

[15] Tracy Borman, *Elizabeth's Women*, p. 209.

[16] *Calendar of State Papers Foreign: Elizabeth,* Volume 2, 1559-1560, n. 5.

[17] Agnes Strickland, *Lives of the Tudor Princesses: Including Lady Jane Gray and Her Sisters*, p. 194.

[18] Ibid., p. 195-96.

[19] The following account of events is based upon BL, Add MS 33749 ("*Transcript of the proceedings, with depositions, etc., of a royal commission to enquire into an alleged marriage between Edward Seymour, Earl of Hertford, and the Lady Catherine Grey; 7 Feb.-12 May, 1562*").

[20] Ibid.

CHAPTER 11: MOTHER OF THE TRAITOR

On 22 August 1561, the news of Lady Katherine Grey's arrest reached the ears of Hertford's mother. Anne Seymour, Duchess of Somerset, immediately wrote a letter to her old acquaintance William Cecil, who had become one of the most powerful men in Elizabethan England. Dipping her quill in the ink, the perplexed duchess wrote:

"Good Master Secretary,

Hearing a great bruit that my Lady Katherine Grey is in the Tower, and also that she should say she is married already to my son, I could not choose but trouble you with my cares and sorrows thereof. And although I might, upon my son's earnest and often protesting unto me the contrary, desire you to be an humble suitor on my behalf, that her tales might not be credited before my son did answer, yet, instead thereof, my first and chief suit is that the Queen's Majesty will think and judge of me, in this matter, according to my desire and meaning. And if my son have so much forgotten her Highness calling him to honour, and so much overshot his bounded duty, and so far abused her Majesty's benignity, yet never was his mother privy or consenting thereunto. I will not fill my letter with how much I have schooled and persuaded him to the contrary, nor yet will desire that youth and fear may help, excuse, or lessen his fault; but only that Her Highness will have that opinion of me as of one that, neither for child nor friend, shall willingly neglect the duty of a faithful subject. And to conserve my credit with Her Majesty, good master Secretary, stand now my friend, that the wildness of mine unruly child do not diminish Her Majesty's favour towards me. And thus so perplexed with this discomfortable rumour, I end, not knowing how to proceed nor what to do therein. Therefore, good master Secretary, let me understand some comfort of my grief from the Queen's Majesty, and some counsel from yourself, and so do leave you to God.

Your assured friend to my power, Anne Somerset."[1]

When Hertford returned from overseas, he was immediately incarcerated in the Tower and examined. During the interrogation, he admitted that his mother didn't know that the marriage took place, but she was well aware that he was in love with Katherine and intended to espouse her. Hertford revealed that Anne, "perceiving the familiarity and goodwill between the Lady Katherine and him, did often admonish him to abstain from her company". Yet

Anne's admonishments made little impression on Hertford, who retorted that "young folks meaning well might well accompany together, and that both in that house [Hanworth] and also in the Court he trusted he might use her [Lady Katherine's] company, being not forbidden by the Queen's highness express commandment".[2]

As the summer faded into autumn, it became painfully clear to all involved in the case that Queen Elizabeth had no intention of forgiving Katherine and Hertford. On 24 September 1561, Katherine gave birth to a son, whom she named Edward, after her husband. The boy was Elizabeth's male successor, but the Queen had no intention of recognizing him as such. She appointed a commission led by Matthew Parker, Archbishop of Canterbury, to enquire into the validity of the marriage. As she explained to Sir Edward Warner, Lieutenant of the Tower, its purpose was to "examine, enquire and judge of the infamous conversation and pretended marriage" of the couple.[3] That Elizabeth used the word "pretended" in relation to her kinswoman's marriage makes it clear that the outcome of the investigation was a foregone conclusion. The Queen was bent on proving that the marriage was invalid and Lady Katherine Grey was a harlot.

The Queen was not in a good mood in the autumn of 1561. She still continued the charade and prolonged the marriage negotiations with various candidates, knowing deep down that she would never consent to any proposal. Foreign ambassadors were not easily fooled, and many believed the Queen was only pretending to be interested. "Here we are, ten or twelve ambassadors, competing for her favour", wrote Ambassador Álvaro de la Quadra, Bishop of Aquila, to the Count of Feria, whom he replaced.[4] It was becoming more and more evident that the Queen would probably never marry, or "if she married at all it would only be to a man whom she knew".[5]

Rumours about her romantic involvement with Robert Dudley gained more currency, and even the Queen's governess, Kat Ashley, felt obliged to urge Elizabeth to put an end to "disreputable rumours" by marrying. Elizabeth said that she had "never understood how any single person could be displeased, seeing that she was always surrounded by her Ladies of the Bedchamber and Maids of Honour, who at all times could see whether there was anything dishonourable between her and her Master of the Horse". She also added that "if she had ever had the will or had found pleasure in such a dishonourable life . . . she did not know of anyone who could forbid her; but she trusted in

God that nobody would ever live to see her so commit herself".[6]

It seemed that Elizabeth was bent on marrying Dudley. She even asked de la Quadra, Philip II's ambassador, "what your Majesty would think if she married one of her servitors as the Duchess of Suffolk and the Duchess of Somerset had done".[7] Elizabeth was referring to the fact that two of the high-ranking peeresses of her realm had married beneath their stations; the late Frances Grey to her Master of the Horse, Adrian Stokes, and Anne Seymour to the former steward of her first husband's household, Francis Newdigate. But Dudley was a scandalous choice for a husband. Not only was he the son of an executed traitor, but his wife, Amy, had been found dead at the bottom of a flight of stairs with a broken neck amid rumours of murder. Whether Amy Dudley was murdered, committed suicide or was the victim of an unfortunate accident is unknowable today.[8] What we do know is that her death in such unclear and suspicious circumstances reflected badly on her husband and the Queen.

Elizabeth continued the subtle marriage game, misleading foreign ambassadors by using her own ladies-in-waiting, who carried secret messages purportedly in the Queen's name to keep the negotiations going without the

Queen taking a direct part in them; Ambassador de la Quadra reported that Elisabeth Parr, Marchioness of Northampton, "has received valuable presents" from the Swedish embassy. At that time, however, Queen Elizabeth's health was deteriorating; in September 1561, she was said to have been "dropsical and has already begun to swell extraordinarily". She was "extremely thin and the colour of a corpse", according to an eyewitness. De la Quadra noticed that Elisabeth Parr and her sister-in-law, Frances Brooke, Lady Cobham, believed that the Queen's condition was serious. "If they are mistaken I am mistaken also", he observed, showing just how close the Marchioness of Northampton was to her royal mistress. Elisabeth Parr was believed to have had an insight into the Queen's opinions about marriage and the state of her health; she was, in the ambassador's own words, "in a better position to judge than anyone else".[9]

If Elizabeth could not marry Robert Dudley, Katherine could not stay married to the Earl of Hertford. In a missive to the Duchess of Parma, de la Quadra wrote:

"The Queen claims that the marriage is not to be considered valid as there was no witness, although both Katharine and the Earl declare they are married. If they do not like to say, however, who were the witnesses, or that any other persons know of the marriage the act will be held illegal. Notwithstanding this, the Queen is not without anxiety about it, and I will not fail to advise your Highness of all that may happen in regard to the business."[10]

Although the marriage certainly took place, the ceremony itself was hushed and irregular. The identity of the priest who officiated was unknown, and the only witness, Lady Jane Seymour, died on 19 March 1561 of consumption. On 12 May 1562, after Katherine and Hertford were vigorously interrogated, their marriage was proclaimed invalid. It followed that their son was illegitimate. Hertford was found guilty of carnal copulation with a woman of royal blood and proclaimed a traitor. Yet public opinion in England was divided. Some agreed that since there were no witnesses, the Queen's decision to dissolve the match was well-founded. Others, however, believed the couple were truly married. Sympathetic guards allowed Katherine and Hertford to spend two nights together in Katherine's chambers in the Tower. Another son, Thomas, was born on 10 February 1563, to the intense rage of Queen Elizabeth. Hertford was heavily fined, and his imprisonment was to continue at the Queen's pleasure.

When the plague broke out in London in the summer of 1563, Queen Elizabeth made sure that Lady Katherine was removed from the Tower and placed far from the outbreak of the illness. She intended to let Hertford rot in the Tower though, but "upon much humble suit" she agreed to release him and his eldest son into the care of his mother at Hanworth.[11] The unnamed humble suitor may have been Anne Seymour herself since she was mad with worry about her precious eldest son and the grandsons she hadn't met yet. Lady Katherine and her younger son, Thomas, were conducted to the estates of her uncle, Sir John Grey, at Pirgo in Essex. The man who escorted her was Sir Francis Newdigate, Anne Seymour's second husband. It seemed that the Queen would soon forgive the couple and allow them to live together with their sons as a family. Lady Katherine certainly thought so, for she wrote a letter of thanks to William Cecil, adding a postscript attesting to her hopes of restoration to the royal favour:

"Thus, resting in prayer for the Queen's Majesty's long reign over us, the forgiveness of mine offence and shortly enjoying the company of mine own dear lord and husband, with assured hope, through God's grace and your good help, and that of my Lord Robert for the enjoying of the Queen's Highness's favour in that behalf, I bid you, mine own good cousin, most heartily farewell."[12]

Katherine also wrote to Hertford, thanking him for his "husbandly concern in enquiring how I am, and in sending me money". "I long to be merry with you, as I know you do with me, as we were when our sweet little boys were gotten in the Tower", she wrote, referring to the passionate nights they spent together in the Tower. She also wrote that she would "willingly bear the pain of further childbirth" only to taste pleasure with her "sweet bedfellow" again. These passages were too racy to be included in the nineteenth-century transcription of the letter[13] but were recently published in a new biography of the Grey sisters.[14] Besides her declarations of love for Hertford, Katherine's letter reveals that Anne Seymour took a great interest in her daughter-in-law: "Now to her Grace, whose letter I send you here inclosed [sic] that you may see how kindly she wrytheth."[15]

Katherine believed that now, after she humbly submitted herself to the Queen and acknowledged her faults, she would be forgiven. Elizabeth, however, was not in a mood to forgive or forget. When it soon became apparent that Katherine's house arrest was going to be longer than she anticipated, the young girl became severely depressed. Katherine's perplexed uncle, who sympathised with her, wrote to William Cecil that she pined away knowing that the Queen's forgiveness was not forthcoming. She refused to eat and spent whole days secluded in her chamber:

"Before God I speak it, if it [the Queen's pardon] cometh not soon she will not live long thus, for she eateth not above six morsels in the meal. I say to her, 'Good Madam, eat somewhat to comfort yourself.' She falls a weeping, and goes up to her chamber. If I ask her 'what the cause is she useth herself in that sort', she answers me, 'Alas! Uncle, what a life is this to me, thus to live in the Queen's displeasure; but for my lord and my children, I would I were buried."[16]

It pained Sir John to see his niece in such a state. "Good cousin Cecil", he urged, "as time, place and occasion may serve, ease her of this woeful grief and sorrow, and rid me of this life, which I assure you grieveth me even at the heart-roots". Cecil, moved by pity, decided to act and convinced Katherine that an abject letter of apology might satisfy the Queen. On 6 November 1563, she wrote to Elizabeth, craving "pardon for my disobedient and rash matching of myself without your Highness's consent".

Describing herself as a "most unworthy creature", Katherine wallowed in self-pity, begging to be restored to Elizabeth's good graces.[17]

Katherine's plea made little impression on the Queen, who didn't send any reply to her heartbroken cousin. On 13 December 1563, Katherine wrote to William Cecil complaining that her prolonged exile had put a mark on "this miserable and wretched body of mine". "I rather wish of God shortly to be buried in the faith and fear of Him, than thus in continual agony to live", she wrote dramatically.[18] Sir John Grey attested to her "miserable and woeful state" and mentioned to Cecil that he thought it wise if the Queen's own physicians visited his niece. Katherine was not even twenty-five yet, but she was ill in body and soul. She was emaciated after persistently refusing to eat, her face and eyes were swollen from constant crying and her mood was becoming increasingly dark. Sir John implied he was afraid she might commit suicide while in his care:

"She is so fraught with phlegm, by reason of thought, weeping and sitting still, that many hours she is like to be overcome therewith; so if she had not careful women about her, I tell you truly, cousin Cecil, I could not sleep in quiet. Thus with my commendations to you, and to my good Lady

Cecil, my cousin, I wish the same quiet of mind as to myself."[19]

Furthermore, the Greys and the Seymours started arguing over the expenses of Katherine's humble establishment. Sir John had to provide everything from the very first day Katherine and her "little boy" Thomas set foot in his house. Sir John clashed with Anne Seymour's husband, Francis Newdigate, who escorted Katherine to Pirgo in September 1563. He was "very plain with Newdigate" about Katherine's expenses, believing that, as Hertford's wife, she should receive money from the Seymours. Sir John received merely £20 for her upkeep "from Hanworth", and in her letter to Hertford, Katherine thanked him for the money. In an angry letter to Cecil, Sir John claimed that the Seymours promised new beds and sheets for Katherine, yet they failed to materialize. Katherine didn't even have money to buy the customary New Year's gifts for her friends in London, Sir John raged. These friends, including Lady Catherine Knollys, the Queen's Boleyn cousin, could intercede on Katherine's behalf with the Queen. Overall, he wrote to Cecil that "the inventory of all she had when Newdigate left her here I could send to you, but I am ashamed, for that it was so bare".[20] Cecil, moved by compassion, asked for Robert

Dudley's help. The two men addressed a joint letter to Hertford, gently urging him to provide a substantial sum of £114 for Katherine's upkeep:

"We have thought good to require you to send someone hither with the said sum of money, which may be sent to Pirgo to Lady Grey, whereat it is necessary that you make some expedition, because the said Lady Grey, as she complaineth, can no longer endure from payment, and so we bid you farewell."[21]

They were careful not to call Katherine Hertford's wife, although she signed her own letters as "Katherine Hertford", signifying her married status to the world. Whereas Katherine sank deeper into depression, Hertford started writing letters to the important personages at court. Among his most prestigious contacts was Robert Dudley, the Queen's favourite and, many whispered, her lover. Under house arrest, Hertford could not leave Hanworth, but his mother could.

During the spring of 1564, the Duchess of Somerset left her luxurious residence and went to court to talk to Dudley in person. She dared not approach the Queen directly, and the custom dictated cultivating the monarch's good graces through her trusted politicians and favourites.

On 18 March, Hertford penned a letter to Dudley, wherein he thanked him "for the friendly welcoming and honourable using of my lady my mother, since her now being at the court, as also your well-tried and goodly noble furthering her long and troublesome suit for us, to our most gracious Queen".[22] Four days later Dudley replied that he petitioned the Queen to grant him pardon, a move that was "not disliked" by Elizabeth. Dudley further added that Hertford's mother "also has done her part".[23]

Dudley's motives for helping Anne Seymour and her son are not entirely clear. Perhaps he felt that he had some sort of a moral obligation towards them since his father executed the Duke of Somerset. In any rate, all attempts to help Katherine were botched when one John Hales decided to write a tract about succession.

Unlike her father and brother, Queen Elizabeth believed that the Stuarts, who sprang from Henry VIII's elder sister, Margaret, had precedence over the descendants of her junior aunt, Mary the French Queen. She thus favoured the claim of Mary Queen of Scots and was willing to designate her as her successor. But Mary was foreign and a Catholic, whereas Katherine Grey was English and Protestant. She naturally had supporters who were unhappy about the Queen's stubborn wish to proclaim her favour for Mary Queen of Scots's claim.

Tired of waiting for the Queen's decision, Sir John Grey and his friend John Hales sent scholar Robert Beal to consult opinions of "learned men" on the Continent concerning the validity of the Grey-Seymour marriage.[24] Hales also wrote a pamphlet about the succession, wherein he argued the superiority of Katherine Grey's claim. Henry VIII's last will should be respected, he argued, and foreigners were banned from inheriting the throne by common law anyway. Hales's pamphlet didn't help Katherine Grey's cause and further infuriated the Queen. "Here is fallen out a troublesome fond matter", William Cecil wrote to Thomas Smith on 27 April 1564. He further explained:

"John Hales had secretly made a book in the time of the last Parliament wherein he hath taken upon himself to discuss no small matter, viz. the title to the Crown after the Queen's Majesty. Having confuted and rejected the line of the Scottish Queen, and made the line of the Lady Frances mother to the Lady Katherine only next and lawful. He is committed to the Fleet for his boldness, especially because he hath communicated it to sundry persons. My Lord John Grey is in trouble also for it. Beside this, John Hales hath procured sentences and counsels of lawyers from beyond seas to be written in maintenance of the Earl of Hertford's marriage. This dealing of his offended the Queen's Majesty very much."[25]

Anne Seymour's husband, Francis Newdigate, communicated with Hales and supported his views concerning the succession and Katherine Grey's place in it. In a letter to William Cecil written on 23 April 1564, Newdigate explained that "the Scottish matter"—Queen Elizabeth's fervent wish to proclaim Mary Queen of Scots as her heiress—was "a hindrance to our suit".[26] Though Newdigate was politically insignificant and had no reason to meddle in such high levels of state matters, it was he who first approached Hales and who sponsored his enterprises. It appears that he did all that on Anne's behalf. Later in his life he would reminisce that he received all his preferment by his marriage to the duchess. After the scandals of the 1550s, Anne could not afford to openly meddle in politics, but her husband could and did. It is clear from his letter to Cecil that Newdigate was working on the duchess's behalf and was voicing her own opinions:

"And after, in talk what was to be done in our suit, I declared my Lady's Grace answers were such at Court for my Lord [Robert Dudley], as I feared some further misliking, and that we should sure hear somewhat done this term by judges and commissionaires, either in this appeal or in this Book Matter; for otherwise surely her Grace should have gotten my Lord to the court."[27]

Hertford's match appears to have been fuelled by true love rather than the wish to become the husband of a politically significant claimant to the throne, but the fact that Katherine Grey was considered by many to be the next in line to Elizabeth's throne certainly added prestige to the marriage. Anne, it appears, still harboured hopes of grand matches for her children. In May 1564, Newdigate wrote to Cecil again, denying rumours that Anne planned to marry one of her daughters into the Swedish royal family.[28] Whether the rumour was true or not, it shows that Anne was still involved in politics. She hoped that the Queen would eventually relent and forgive her son and his wife.

NOTES

[1] Agnes Strickland, *Lives of the Tudor Princesses: Including Lady Jane Gray and Her Sisters*, p. 210.
[2] BL, Add MS 33749.
[3] Ibid.
[4] *Calendar of State Papers, Spain (Simancas),* Volume 1, 1558-1567, n. 70.
[5] Ibid., n. 64.

[6] Victor von Klarwill (ed.), *Queen Elizabeth and Some Foreigners*, pp. 113-15.
[7] *Calendar of State Papers, Spain (Simancas)*, Volume 1, 1558-1567, n. 123.
[8] In *Death and the Virgin: Elizabeth, Dudley and the Mysterious Fate of Amy Robsart*, historian Chris Skidmore tried to solve this historical mystery, examining the coroner's report found in 2008. For a comprehensive study of Amy's brief life and death see also Christine Hartweg's *Amy Robsart: A Life and Its End*.
[9] *Calendar of State Papers, Spain (Simancas)*, Volume 1, 1558-1567, n. 139.
[10] Ibid., n. 140.
[11] Samuel Haynes, *A Collection of State Papers*, p. 405.
[12] Agnes Strickland, *Lives of the Tudor Princesses: Including Lady Jane Gray and Her Sisters*, p. 230.
[13] "A few sentences . . . of a purely private kind I have withheld", wrote reverend John Edward Jackson, editor of *Wulfhall and the Seymours*.
[14] Leanda de Lisle, *Sisters Who Would Be Queen*, p. 242.
[15] "Her Grace" mentioned in the letter cannot be Queen Elizabeth, as she never contacted Katherine directly. John Edward Jackson, *Wulfhall and the Seymours*, p. 35.
[16] Agnes Strickland, *Lives of the Tudor Princesses: Including Lady Jane Gray and Her Sisters*, p. 232.
[17] Ibid., p. 233-234.
[18] Ibid., p. 230.
[19] Ibid., p. 235.
[20] Ibid., p. 238.
[21] Ibid., p. 240.
[22] Ibid., p. 241.
[23] Samuel Haynes, *A Collection of State Papers*, p. 236.
[24] Ibid., p. 406.
[25] Henry Ellis, *Original Letters Illustrative of English History*, Volume 2 (2nd series), p. 285.
[26] Samuel Haynes, *A Collection of State Papers*, p. 411.
[27] Ibid., 412.
[28] *Calendar of State Papers*, p. 241.

CHAPTER 12: DEATH OF A MARCHIONESS

Elisabeth Parr, Marchioness of Northampton, was in a good position to intercede with the Queen on behalf of Katherine Grey and the Earl of Hertford. Unfortunately, her health was deteriorating. In 1562, she suffered from jaundice and high fever. "Almighty God comfort her, and permit us to enjoy her for I think none shall be more grievously lost of a subject of this Court", wrote the Queen's secretary, William Cecil.[1] Early in 1564, it became apparent that the marchioness, aged thirty-eight, was suffering from a "disease in one of her breasts" (breast cancer), and she immediately started seeking professional medical help. Yet she soon realised that the English physicians had no expertise in dealing with such serious ailments, and Elisabeth sought permission to depart to the Netherlands. Queen Elizabeth immediately agreed that the marchioness's disease "can be cured only in the Low Countries", and wrote a letter to Margaret, Duchess of Parma, Regent of the Netherlands, requesting safe passage for Elisabeth, who was accompanied by her brother William Brooke, Lord Cobham, and his wife, Frances. In the letter, Queen

Elizabeth referred to the Marchioness of Northampton not merely as her friend but as "our dearest cousin".[2]

The party arrived in Antwerp by 12 April 1564. Elisabeth's brother wrote to William Cecil, the Queen's secretary, informing him that since their arrival his sister had physicians and surgeons attending to her, but they could not agree on how to approach her illness. They were to confer for two days and deliver their opinions in writing and decide upon the method of treatment.[3] Yet no successful cure was found for the marchioness in the Netherlands. She returned to England in May 1564, escorted by Queen Elizabeth's astrologer, Dr John Dee. Yet neither Elisabeth nor the Queen gave up hope, however. Queen Elizabeth requested the physician who treated the marchioness to come to England to continue in his endeavours. Since this doctor was the private physician of Maximilian II, King of Bohemia and future Holy Roman Emperor, Queen Elizabeth wrote to him, begging him to send Dr Michael to England.

After her return from the Netherlands, Elisabeth spent most of her time secluded in her private apartments at court. The new Spanish ambassador, Don Diego Guzmán de Silva, visited her in September 1564. Writing to

Margaret, Duchess of Parma, Regent of the Netherlands, he included a pen portrait of Elisabeth:

"As your Highness knows the Marchioness of Northampton is a great favourite of the Queen, and I am gaining the goodwill of her intimates, so as to gain more influence over her mistress. She is a person of great understanding, and is so much esteemed by the Queen that some little friction exists between her and Robert [Dudley]. I understand, however, that she bears herself towards him in a way that together with other things that can be better imagined than described make me doubt sometimes whether Robert's position is so irregular as many think. It is nothing for princes to hear evil, even without giving any cause for it."[4]

The ambassador went on to relate how he visited Elisabeth one evening at Westminster Palace, where she had her own lodgings. The ambassador did not know that the marchioness had also invited the Queen, who came especially from St James's Palace, and with whom the marchioness dined "almost alone". "They played me this trick between them and kept the secret until I was in the Queen's presence, and then laughed greatly at it", he recalled. Elisabeth Parr sat on her couch, and the Queen was near her; they talked, laughed and had a great time.

"What passed were mostly tales told by the Queen and ordinary conversation, into which she was constantly slipping some slight allusions to marriage", de Silva remembered.[5] The fact that this political conversation occurred in Elisabeth Parr's lodgings testifies to her close relationship with the Queen.

This was the last mention of Elisabeth Parr in state documents. Despite spending vast amounts of money on her treatment, the marchioness succumbed to breast cancer and died on 2 April 1565, aged only thirty-nine. The Queen paid for her lavish funeral at St Paul's Cathedral. Unfortunately, the cathedral itself was destroyed during the Great Fire of London in 1666. But whereas the marchioness's burial place is no longer extant, a monument enshrined in verse still survives. A ballad entitled "A proper new ballad in praise of my Lady Marquess, whose death is bewailed" was written by William Elderton shortly after Elisabeth's death. It depicts Elisabeth as an ornament to Queen Elizabeth's court ("the fairest flower of my garland"), a woman whose premature death cruelly snatched her from her friends. The author referred to Elisabeth's marriage to William Parr ("whose courting need not be told") and bemoaned the fact that the couple were childless ("whose like now lives not to behold"). The ballad depicts Elisabeth as a universally beloved woman who spared no efforts in helping her friends:

> "Methinks I see her sorrowful tears,
>
> To princely state approaching nye,
>
> Methinks I see her trembling fears,
>
> Lest any her suits should hit awry;
>
> Methinks she should be still in place,
>
> A pitiful speaker to a Queen,
>
> Bewailing every poor man's case,
>
> As many a time she hath been seen."[6]

Five months after Elisabeth's death, a young gentlewoman named Helena von Snakenbourg arrived in England in the train of Princess Cecilia of Sweden. The Spanish ambassador reported: "On the 11th instant the King of Sweden's sister entered London at two o'clock in the afternoon. She is very far advanced in pregnancy, and was dressed in a black velvet robe with a mantle of black cloth of silver, and wore on her head a golden crown . . . She had with her six ladies dressed in crimson taffeta with mantles of the same. She was received at Dover by Lord and

Lady Cobham, the latter of whom is mistress of the robes to the Queen".[7]

William Parr took an instant liking to Helena, whom he called "Elin", an anglicised version of her name, and often talked to her when she accompanied her royal mistress to court. In a letter to her mother, Helena wrote: "Amongst the gentlemen was a courtier who always came with the earliest arrivals and left amongst the last. When my gracious Lady had been 'churched' after the baby was born, the Marquis of Northampton (for that was the Courtier's name) talked to my gracious lady about me."[8] By early 1566, it was well known at court that "my Lord Marquis was suitor, and ensured to one of the Swedish lady's women, and had given her divers jewels". Yet William soon started regretting his decision; "he now hath repented, saying he had another wife [Anne Bourchier] alive, and would have his jewels, but he cannot get them".[9]

As would soon become clear to everyone, Queen Elizabeth was not at all happy about William's hasty decision to remarry so soon after Elisabeth's death. In November 1566, William was among a delegation of nobles who were sent to Queen Elizabeth to urge her to take a husband for the royal succession's sake. "The Queen was so angry", reported the imperial ambassador, that she publicly rebuked the lords. She was especially angry with Parr since she knew he was courting Helena: "She said that Northampton was of no account, and he had better talk about the arguments used to enable him to get married again, when he had a wife living, instead of mincing words with her."[10] The loss of Elisabeth Parr was still fresh in the Queen's memory, and she was furious that William presumed to broach the subject of marriage with her. Still, the Queen liked Helena and retained her as her own maid of honour when Princess Cecilia left England.

Indeed, the loss of Elisabeth Parr was a heavy blow to her family, especially her brother William, Baron Cobham, and his wife, Frances. In 1567, Baron Cobham commissioned a family portrait, now at Longleat House. It was painted by a Netherlandish painter known as A.W., also called the Master of the Countess of Warwick. This family portrait depicting William, Frances, six of their small children and Elisabeth Parr, "appears to have been a joint project by William and Frances, intended at once to celebrate their life together and to create a visual family memorial to their late sister, the Marchioness of Northampton".[11] Which one of the two women is Elisabeth Parr in this portrait is a matter of dispute among historians, but one thing remains certain: it was a celebration of family and a posthumous tribute to Elisabeth.

When William Parr's first wife, Anne Bourchier, died in January 1571, he renewed his courtship of Helena von Snakenbourg. The couple married in May 1571. Queen Elizabeth clearly approved of the match at this stage since Helena had become one of her favourite maids of honour and Anne Bourchier's death removed a legal obstacle to Parr's new marriage. The marriage lasted for five months; William Parr died unexpectedly on 28 October 1571. He had no children by any of his three wives. After Parr's death, William Camden recorded: "Children he had none, but left for his heir Henry Herbert, Earl of Pembroke, his nephew by one of his sisters".[12] His body was laid to rest in St. Mary's Church in Warwick. An inscription on William's tomb says that he was "buried with the ceremonial due of a Knight of the Garter to the Order of Queen Elizabeth who bore the expense of the funeral, 2 December 1571."

NOTES

1 Helen Graham-Matheson, 'Elisabeth Parr's Renaissance at the Mid-Tudor Court', *Early Modern Women*, Vol. 8 (Fall 2013), pp. 289-299.

2 SP 70/70 f. 9: Queen Elizabeth to Margaret, Duchess of Parma [*Calendar of State Papers Foreign: Elizabeth, Volume 7, 1564-1565*, n. 287.]

[3] SP 12/33 f. 61: William Brooke, Lord Cobham to William Cecil, 12 April 1564.

[4] *Calendar of State Papers, Spain (Simancas),* Volume 1, 1558-1567, n. 267.

[5] Ibid.

[6] Victor E. Neuburg, *Popular Literature, a History and Guide: From the Beginning of Printing to the Year 1897*, pp. 28-30.

[7] *Calendar of State Papers, Spain (Simancas),* Volume 1, 1558-1567, n. 320.

[8] Charles Angell Bradford, *Helena, Marchioness of Northampton,* p. 48.

[9] *HMC, Salisbury,* Volume 1, p. 326.

[10] *Calendar of State Papers, Spain (Simancas),* Volume 1, 1558-1567, n. 388.

[11] Susan E. James, *The Feminine Dynamic in English Art, 1485-1603: Women as Consumers, Patrons and Painters*, p. 51.

[12] William Camden, *The History of the Most Renowned and Victorious Princess Elizabeth Late Queen of England*, p. 169.

Chapter 13: This Tedious Suit

In the aftermath of Hales's "foolish attempt in writing the book so precisely against the Queen of Scotland's title", Queen Elizabeth removed the Earl of Hertford from under his mother's care and placed him with the unsympathetic jailor Sir James Mason. "The Queen's displeasure continued still towards my Lord of Hertford and the Lady Katherine", William Cecil wrote to Thomas Smith on 30 December 1564. Katherine Grey also switched residences after her uncle died on 20 November. In a letter to Thomas Smith, William Cecil wrote that Sir John Grey's friends believed that he died "of thought"—depression. Yet the pragmatic Cecil preferred to find another explanation, one that weighted less heavily on his own conscience, and surmised that "his gout was sufficient to have ended his life".[1]

Anne, Duchess of Somerset, still had her precious grandson Edward, Lord Beauchamp, in her care, but she could not understand Queen Elizabeth's cruelty in separating Hertford and Katherine Grey. In January 1565, Anne decided to write directly to Queen Elizabeth. She explained that hadn't wanted to bother the Queen earlier but now felt compelled to write:

"And herewithal for that I have so long forborne to molest your Majesty touching the tedious suit of my son, and for all that wisdom wisheth I should not still shut up my sorrows in silence, I cannot but presume your Majesty's godly nature will bear with a mother's most humble petition which is that among all your merciful and virtuous proceedings in all causes and towards all persons, the lamentable state and case of my son may not alone be without all favour and forgiveness and herein for me to remember this more than four years' imprisonment, the great and importable fine or other their worse griefs of mind, as punishment worthy for their offences, or that since their delivery, any more than the first fault of disordered love by any trial can justly be found I will not, but setting all excusing and justifying apart, fully and wholly depend on your Majesty's mercy, which the sooner your Highness shall witsafe to extend, the more they must stand bound in all services to do what in them may lie to recompense some part of their former offences, and so do rest in prayer for your Majesty's long preservation wishing God to make your Highness mother of some sweet prince to the end your

Majesty might the better conceive what a mother's cares and affection can mean."[2]

At the same time, Anne wrote yet another beseeching letter to her old acquaintance William Cecil. She was disappointed at the Queen's treatment of her son and his wife and hoped something would change and soon, for Katherine was sliding deeper into depression. It was unthinkable that such a young couple should waste their lives in prison, the duchess reasoned. Bitter disappointment is palpable in her letter:

"Good Master Secretary,

After this long silence, and for that, as yet, mine old occasion lets [hinders] mine attendance, I have presumed by letter to renew my suit for my son to the Queen's Majesty, and have likewise written to my Lord of Leicester [Robert Dudley], praying you to set in your helping hand to end this tedious suit; wherein for me to reason how much her Highness' displeasure is too long lasting, or how unmet it is this young couple should thus wax old in prison, or how far better it were for them to be abroad and learn to serve, I will not say; but leave those and like speeches to the friendly setting forth of my lord [Dudley] and you. Only my seeking is, that as there is none other cause, but hath some favourable order or end since her Majesty's reign, so by your earnest conferring and joining with my good lord, this young couple may feel somelike of her Majesty's plentiful mercy; to the procurement whereof, the more earnest my lord and you shall show yourselves, the more shall you set forth the Queen's Majesty's honour, and, as a mother, I must needs say, the better discharge your calling and credit. And so, resting in prayer that God would bless your travail to some comfortable end, I take my leave.

Your assured loving friend,

Anne Somerset."[3]

Despite Anne's fears that her son and daughter-in-law would "wax old in prison", two portraits of the couple painted at the time of their incarceration still survive. Hertford's portrait dates to 1565 and shows a dashingly handsome twenty-six-year-old wearing a white doublet with a high-standing collar adorned with a ruff. Hanging over his left shoulder is a black coat; the earl's right hand rests firmly on his dagger. While the young man in the portrait exudes confidence, he was far from confident in real life, complaining of "the great hurt this emprisonment [sic] doth to my health".[4] Katherine was also painted, presumably by Levina Teerlinc, Flemish miniaturist of

Queen Elizabeth's court. The miniature shows Katherine holding her infant son and wearing a miniature of Hertford suspended from a ribbon around her neck. The boy is often said to be her elder son, Beauchamp, although it is more likely that he is Thomas, Katherine's younger son, whom she was allowed to keep with her.

William Cecil strongly supported Katherine Grey's claim to the throne and believed that her sons, even after being proclaimed illegitimate, could still be Elizabeth's heirs. After all, the Queen herself had been illegitimate when she assumed the throne. He was apparently very vocal in his support of the Grey-Seymour marriage since, in a letter to Smith, he said that he was "somewhat in disgrace for the part he had already taken as their advocate with the Queen".[5] Elizabeth stubbornly pressed for her councillors to accept Mary Queen of Scots as her heiress. She was even willing to arrange a marriage between Robert Dudley and the Scottish Queen in order to control Mary, of whom she was becoming increasingly jealous. To add more splendour to Robert's name, Elizabeth conferred the earldom of Leicester upon him in September 1564. "My Lord Robert is made Earl of Leicester, and his preferment in Scotland is earnestly intended", Cecil wrote to Thomas Smith on 4 October.[6] Yet the Scottish Queen had no intention of marrying Elizabeth's Master of the Horse and preferred another nobleman of the Queen's court: Henry, Lord Darnley, the son of Elizabeth's first cousin, Margaret Douglas, Countess of Lennox.

During Easter of 1565, Anne Seymour wrote to Cecil again. She apologised for not writing to him earlier, explaining that she sought Robert Dudley's assistance "to whom as I have now written to take some occasion to do good in my son's cause". Anne asked Cecil to work with Robert to achieve obtaining the Queen's pardon for Hertford and Katherine. Anne hoped that "the occasion of this Holy Week and charitable time of forgiveness earnestly set forth by his Lordship and you, will bring forth some comfortable fruit of relief to the long afflicted parties". "I can no more but once again pray your earnest dealing herein", she concluded.[7]

In July 1565, Mary Queen of Scots married Lord Darnley. On 19 June 1566, she gave birth to their son, James. Elizabeth's subjects now believed that their Queen would settle the succession issue during the Parliament in October 1566, but Elizabeth had no intention of doing so. She desperately wanted to avoid having to name her heir, fearing that "if she declared a successor, it would cost much blood to England."[8] It is clear that the Queen had no intention of naming a successor during her lifetime, but she was adamant that if anything happened to her, it would be Mary Queen of Scots and not Katherine Grey who would succeed her. Yet Elizabeth's carefully laid plan was destroyed when the Scottish Queen's husband was murdered in February 1567. Lord Darnley, the "long lad" with feminine features who had appealed to Mary Stuart's refined taste three years earlier, degenerated into an abusive drunkard who allied himself with his wife's enemies. When Darnley's house at Kirk o' Field was blown up and his naked body was found with marks of strangulation on it in the nearby orchard, many pointed accusatory fingers at the Queen of Scots.

Robert Dudley and his camp certainly believed that Mary Stuart stood behind Darnley's murder. Dudley had previously shown signs of accepting the Scottish Queen as Elizabeth's heiress, but the murder of Darnley made him change his mind. "On the night that the King of Scotland's death was known here Lord Robert sent his brother [Ambrose] the Earl of Warwick to the Earl of Hertford, Katherine's husband, to offer him his services in the matter of succession", wrote the Spanish ambassador de Silva, adding that "Lord Robert himself went to see the Duchess of

Somerset, the Earl's mother, with the same object, and had made friends with both of them".[9]

Mary Stuart made a poor choice of her next husband and married James Hepburn, Earl of Bothwell, the main suspect in Darnley's murder. Queen Elizabeth was stunned: "How could a worse choice be made for your honour than in such haste to marry such a subject, who besides other and notorious lacks, public fame hath charged with the murder of your late husband, beside touching of yourself also in some part, though we trust that in that behalf falsely".[10] Mary's actions triggered a rebellion in Scotland. The Queen was deposed by her own subjects, who imprisoned her in Loch Leven Castle and crowned her son, James, on 29 July 1567.

Elizabeth feared that Katherine Grey's camp was "strong and might cause trouble".[11] She now wanted to help Mary Stuart reclaim her lost throne. As to Katherine and Hertford, they were to continue languishing under house arrest. "I am informed that they have again increased the strictness with which they have imprisoned the Earl of Hertford, Katherine's husband", de Silva wrote in December 1567.[12] Katherine was also under strict guard, a virtual prisoner who could neither venture outside nor join dinner when her hosts had guests. Katherine's newest jailor was Sir Owen Hopton, who lived at Cockfield Hall in Suffolk.

Five years into her imprisonment, the twenty-seven-year-old Katherine looked like a shadow of her former self. She used to be a beautiful blonde with clear blue eyes and milky complexion, but after years of refusing proper nourishment, she looked pale and emaciated. In early January 1568, her fragile health began to deteriorate. As soon as Sir Owen noticed Katherine's illness, he urged William Cecil to fetch the Queen's physician. Katherine's servants believed she would shake off her malady. "Madam, be of good cheer", they said, "with God's help you shall live and do well many years". "No, no", Katherine replied, "no life in this world; but in the world to come I hope to live forever: for here is nothing but care and misery, and there is life everlasting".

At night, as she felt the strength leaving her body, Katherine prayed incessantly, repeating the orisons in the *Book of Common Prayer*, the service for the Visitation of the Sick from the same and the Psalms. When she fainted, her attendants started rubbing her to restore her consciousness, but Katherine would lift up her hands and eyes and say, "Father of Heaven, for thy Son Christ's sake, have mercy upon me!"

Sir Owen's wife, Lady Hopton, endeavoured to persuade her that she would live, saying, "Madam, be of good comfort, for with God's favour you shall live and escape this; for Mrs Cousins said you have escaped many dangers when you were as like to die as you are now". But Katherine was reconciled to the idea of death. "No, no, my lady", she said, "my time is come, and it is not God's will I should live longer. His will be done, not mine".

At six or seven o'clock in the morning, Katherine summoned Sir Owen to her bedside. When he asked her about her health, she said that she was "going to God" and wished the assembled to witness that she died a "true Christian". Desperate to die with a clear conscience, she asked "God and all the world forgiveness", adding that she forgave "all the world". She charged Sir Owen with one last task:

"I beseech you promise me one thing, that you yourself, with your own mouth, will make this request unto the Queen's Majesty, which shall be the last suit and request I ever shall make to her Highness, even from the mouth of a dead woman, that she would forgive her displeasure towards me, as my hope is she had done. I must needs confess I have greatly offended her, in that I made my choice without her knowledge, otherwise I take God to witness, I had never the heart to think any evil against Her Majesty; and that she would be good unto my children, and not impute my fault unto them, whom I give wholly to her Majesty; for in my life they have had few friends, and fewer shall they have when I am dead, except her Majesty be gracious unto them; and I desire her Highness to be good unto my Lord Hertford, for I know this, my death, will be heavy news to him; that her Grace will be so good as to send liberty to glad his sorrowful heart withal."

She tasked Sir Owen to give her husband a ring with a pointed diamond, the same that she received from Hertford when he asked her to marry him. "What say you, Madam?" Sir Owen asked, "was this your wedding ring?" The sole existence of such a ring implied that Katherine's marriage was valid. She replied that this was the ring of "my assurance to Lord Hertford", an engagement ring. She pulled another one from her jewel box, saying, "there is my wedding ring". She further instructed Sir Owen:

"Deliver this also to my lord, and pray him, even as I have been to him (as I take God to witness I have been) a true and a faithful wife, that he will be a loving and natural father to our children, to whom I give the same blessing that God gave unto Abraham, Isaac and Jacob."

There was one last gift for Hertford. "This shall be the last token to my lord that ever I shall send him; it is the picture of myself". She pulled another ring, mounted with a death's head with an engraved motto: "While I lived, yours". Looking down at her bony hands, Katherine noticed her fingernails were turning purple. "Welcome death!" she exclaimed joyfully. "O Lord! Into thy hands I commend my spirit", she said piously and closed her eyes with her own hands in a dramatic gesture. She died at nine o'clock on 27 January 1568.[13]

The imperial ambassador de Silva reported that the "heretics" mourned Katherine's loss "as they had fixed their eyes on her for the succession in any eventuality". In a conversation with the ambassador, Queen Elizabeth "expressed sorrow" at Katherine's death, but de Silva suspected that this was just a façade. "It is not believed that she feels it, as she was afraid of her", he observed.[14] Elizabeth paid for the funeral expenses, but Katherine was buried as she lived: quietly and without pomp. Her two sons, aged six and four, were entrusted to the care of Anne, Duchess of Somerset.

Katherine's hope that her death would set Hertford free proved to be futile. In the summer of 1571, he was still complaining to Cecil (now Baron Burghley) of "his continued sorrow for want of the Queen's favour".[15] He was eventually released after ten years, but the fine imposed on him was crippling, and it wasn't until the 1590s that Hertford was reintegrated into society.

But Katherine was far from forgotten. In October 1572, Queen Elizabeth was reportedly "very ill and the malady proved to be smallpox". The Queen had survived smallpox ten years earlier, but the skin on her face still carried reminders of that near-death experience. Now, as she lay feverish in her bed, her councillors had once again sought to settle the succession. They agreed that if the Queen died, she should be succeeded by "one of the two sons of the earl of Hertford by Lady Katherine . . . The two boys are being brought up by their paternal grandmother, the Duchess of Somerset".[16]

Anne took her role seriously and put much effort into raising her grandsons, but, as she was soon to discover, one of them was as spirited and unruly as his father.

NOTES

[1] Thomas Wright (ed.), *Queen Elizabeth and Her Times*, Volume 1, p. 180-184.
[2] *HMC, Pepys,* Volume 70, p. 73.
[3] Henry Ellis, *Original Letters Illustrative of English History*, Volume 2 (2nd series), p. 286-287.
[4] Marjorie Blatcher (ed.), *The Seymour Papers 1532-1686*, p. 178.
[5] Henry Ellis, *Original Letters Illustrative of English History*, Volume 2 (2nd series), p. 286-287.
[6] Thomas Wright (ed.), *Queen Elizabeth and Her Times*, Volume 1, p. 177.
[7] Henry Ellis, *Original Letters Illustrative of English History*, Volume 2 (2nd series), p. 288.
[8] *Calendar of State Papers, Spain (Simancas)*, Volume 1, n. 211.
[9] Ibid., n. 407.
[10] Janel Mueller, *Elizabeth I: Collected Works*, p. 118.
[11] *Calendar of State Papers, Spain (Simancas)*, Volume 1, n. 408.
[12] Ibid., n. 458.
[13] Agnes Strickland, *Lives of the Tudor Princesses: Including Lady Jane Gray and Her Sisters*, p. 249-253.
[14] *Calendar of State Papers, Spain (Simancas)*, Volume 2, 1568-1579, n. 5.
[15] Samuel Haynes, *A Collection of State Papers, Relating to Affairs in the Reigns of King Henry VIII. King Edward VI, Queen Mary, and Queen Elizabeth from 1542-1570*, p. 415.
[16] *Calendar of State Papers, Spain (Simancas)*, Volume 2, 1568-1579, n. 356.

CHAPTER 14: THE DUCHESS'S LAST YEARS

Hertford's treason didn't diminish Anne Seymour's standing with Queen Elizabeth. In 1575, she was given back Somerset House, the opulent residence on the Strand built by her first husband. Two years later she wrote to William Cecil, recommending one "Mr Druse for preferment", a sign that she was still influential.[1] Hertford eventually recovered his standing with the Queen, doubtless because Elizabeth liked and favoured his mother. At New Year of 1580, the Queen showed Hertford that she wore his "last year's New Year's gift hanging at her girdle". "I told her she did me very great honour in the wearing and that she was worthy of a better favour", he told her and promised to obtain for her a fine jewel he had seen recently, possibly in his mother's vast collection.[2] The Seymours exchanged New Year's gifts with the Queen each year. In 1579, the Duchess of Somerset and her daughters Mary and Elizabeth, as well as Hertford, all presented the Queen with lavish gifts.[3] In August 1580, the duchess dined with the Queen at court and a year later wrote to Cecil again, this time requesting that her nephew (son of her executed half brother), Edward Stanhope, become the new Master of Requests.[4]

In 1581, Anne's grandson, the twenty-year-old Edward Seymour, recently created Viscount Beauchamp despite his illegitimacy, fell in love with Honora Rogers. Honora served at Hanworth and belonged to a wide network of the Seymour kith and kin. Her brother, Sir Andrew Rogers, was married to one of the Duchess of Somerset's daughters, Mary. Beauchamp and Honora kept their relationship secret, but when Hertford eventually found out about it, he was furious.

Honora, he bluntly told his elder son, was not a woman for him. He scathingly referred to her as "Onus Blouse", a derogatory pun on the match meaning a "burdensome trull" or "fat, red-faced wench", the latter phrase giving an idea of what Honora may have looked like.[5] Hertford forbade his son to marry Honora, insisting that she was an "unwholesome woman" and saying that her reputation was damaged. Anne Seymour herself dismissed Honora, saying that "she was but a baggage, though she had served her two years at her father's charge". Others, Hertford claimed, called Honora a "whore" and even his son, in love as he appeared to have been, sought only "one night's lodging with her" in the beginning.[6]

Honora, who admittedly had a "good wit", had an ally in the person of her brother's wife, Mary, Anne Seymour's daughter. Mary appears to have been Beauchamp's favourite aunt, with whom he often exchanged correspondence. In April 1579, for instance, he addressed her as his "loving Aunt" and comforted her in her "great heaviness" after she lost her child.[7] It was natural for Mary to take the part of the couple's advocate. Mary's husband, Andrew, was said to encourage Beauchamp in his pursuit of Honora, and he talked about their relationship openly in Mary's chambers with Honora present. The Duchess of Somerset shared Hertford's views that Honora was an inappropriate a match for Beauchamp, and when she started suspecting that the two were a couple, she "committed the whole examination" to Mary, who "reported all well", apparently obscuring some facts so as not to displease her mother.[8]

Hertford's reaction to his son's secret relationship seems absurd considering that he himself made a secret love match in 1561. But he married an heiress to the throne and hoped that his sons would also match themselves with illustrious ladies to further their claims to the throne. In fact, Hertford saw Beauchamp's secret marriage as a betrayal of Katherine Grey's memory. It had been thirteen years since Katherine's death, but Hertford, despite being in a new relationship, was not ready to move on. His new love interest was Frances Howard, who, like Katherine Grey, was the Queen's kinswoman, though not an heiress to the throne. Born in 1554, Frances was a daughter of William Howard, Baron Howard of Effingham, and his second wife, Margaret Gamage. Frances was one of Queen Elizabeth's numerous favourites, not only because she was sweet-natured and kind, but also because she was her maternal relative.[9]

Hertford had secretly pledged himself to Frances, who was deeply in love with him, signing her letters as his "wife" and referring to his sons as their "mother", although she was only seven years older than Beauchamp. Frances took it upon herself to gently heal the rift between father and son and tried to convince Beauchamp to marry someone of his rank. Addressing him as her "good lord son", she wrote:

"I am sure you know from whence you are descended. Let not a base mind possess so honourable a person: make your choice like unto yourself. Remember the care your lord father has had for your upbringing, be unto him a comfort and God will increase you in all goodness."[10]

Beauchamp was driven by love for Honora and chose her above his natal family. On 15 December 1581, Honora wrote to Beauchamp that "according to your commandment I will not hide from my friends our betrothing any longer".[11] By the end of the month, Anne Seymour found out about the secret engagement and was highly displeased. Her husband, Francis, wrote to Hertford that the elderly duchess "would like to receive your sons to see what good may be done to profit their learning and virtuous exercises and to learn the truth from them of this last brabble which, as it was begun here [at Hanworth], she would do her best to end here". In the same letter, Francis wrote that Anne's health was "after her wonted weak state", suggesting that the duchess, now in her seventies, had health problems. Francis was ailing as well, for he died on 26 January 1582. In his last will, he acknowledged that he owed his social elevation to Anne and bequeathed everything to her: "Since I have received all my preferment by the Duchess's marriage, so I bequeath her all I am able to give her, goods, leases, chattels, plate, jewels, cattle, household stuff, debts, and all land both freehold and copyhold."[12]

In June 1582, Anne "remaineth still troubled with the cough which with her age maketh her feeble and weak".

Ailing though she was, the duchess enjoyed her usual pleasures. She still kept an open house, inviting her neighbours and friends to sup on venison, although her concerned family and servants, who carefully monitored her health, all agreed that venison was "no meat for Her Grace being as she is". Anne's eyesight was failing at this time as evidenced by a golden case for spectacles among her possessions.[13] This did not stop the duchess from enjoying a good read though. She employed her grandsons, Thomas and Beauchamp, in reading letters and books to her. Robert Tutt, who served as tutor to Anne's grandsons, wrote to Hertford:

"Touching my Lord Beauchamp and Mr. Thomas, they continue for their dispositions after one sort. They have read my fellow Smith's last letters in Latin, to Her Grace; and afterwards put the same into English to her Grace, as your Lordship willed. With my Lord Beauchamp Her Grace had special speeches, to what effect I know not, but without all doubt for his great good if he have a prepared mind to follow grave and sound counsels. Her Grace made him fetch his book, entitled, 'Regula Vitae,' & out of the same to read the chapters *'De veritate et mendaciis.'* Your Lordship shall do well in wonted manner to acknowledge her Grace's great care of them and their well doing."[14]

Anne's "special speeches" with Beauchamp certainly concerned his relationship with Honora. The duchess was still against the match, so much so that she argued with her daughter Mary about it and refused to see her when Mary visited her mother at Hanworth. Some people even fed the duchess lies about Mary. The rift between mother and daughter was apparently serious since, on 4 September 1582, Mary wrote to William Cecil, Lord Burghley, asking him to intercede on her behalf with the duchess:

"I have often troubled you with my desires in dealing with my lady Grace for me, so will I continue the same course, knowing by your lordship's means I shall soonest prevail. If in any respect I had forgotten the duty of a child, or dutifully every way had not sought the favour of so dear a parent (as I have ever found her Grace towards me), I would not have relied on your lordship's help. I know many suggestions have been preferred to her Grace behind my back, whereof none will be justified in truth to my face. I was at Hanworth since I saw your lordship last, but my hap was not then so good as to obtain speech of her Grace's own mouth. Minding this week to go again, I desire your lordship to make me the messenger of some [of] your few lines, that I may be accepted to see and speak with her Grace."[15]

The Seymour family drama continued that autumn when Hertford seized Beauchamp and forcibly put him in his custody. On 28 September 1582, Beauchamp wrote to Sir Francis Walsingham, the Queen's secretary and spymaster, complaining that "being with my father is some trouble to his lordship and great disquiet to myself". He apologized if his secret marriage caused offence to the Queen and initially begged Walsingham to help him regain his father's favour, writing: "If my fault is only to my father, I request you to deal with him so that I may recover his favour and to avoid further occasion of dislike to deliver me from his custody."[16] Walsingham, who made a copy of the original, gave the letter to Hertford. On the parchment, Hertford wrote that he sent the letter to his mother so she could see what Beauchamp had done.

In November, Beauchamp wrote to his father, trying to mend their relationship: "I hope that God will mollify your mislike and turn a father's anger into a fatherly remorse." He defended his marriage to Honora and hoped that Hertford would finally accept her as his daughter-in-law. A hint that the Duchess of Somerset still shared

Hertford's opinion and was displeased with her daughter Mary for abetting Beauchamp in his folly is glimpsed in a letter by Roger Puleston to Hertford, wherein he wrote that during the New Year at Hanworth, Mary gave her mother a gift but received nothing in return.[17] The rift between mother and daughter was apparently healed by August 1585, when Mary wrote to Hertford that "her Grace is in health and goes once or twice a week to the Court about your suits and is very well used of all sorts."[18]

Beauchamp was eventually released from his father's custody. In June 1585, Honora gave birth to their first child, a son also named Edward. It appears that the birth of a great-grandson melted the Duchess of Somerset's anger away, and she finally accepted Honora as Beauchamp's wife. Hertford, however, was still angry and made an attempt to nullify Beauchamp's marriage. He received a sharp reply from the Archbishop of Canterbury, who rebuked him, saying that "Christian charity required forgiveness". Hertford still sought to place Beauchamp in his custody, but the Queen strongly opposed such an idea. In a letter to Hertford, his fiancée, Frances Howard, wrote that she spoke with the Queen, who said that "she could not tell what harm he [Beauchamp] might do to himself or others and that he had said when he was taken that he would kill himself rather than stay with you". Frances defended Hertford, saying that it was not his nature to be so cruel and that these rumours were untrue. Queen Elizabeth refused to believe it, saying that "she was sure it was true". Frances urged Hertford to drop the matter: "Therefore, sweet lord, I think it best that you desire no more to have him and in my opinion you are happy to have him thus taken away from you." Frances encouraged Hertford to think about his own happiness since the Queen had finally agreed to give her consent to their marriage: "I trust in God to bring you another pretty boy. Sweet lord, you may have me now when you will, for the Queen praised you and said with all her heart you should have me."[19] By the time Anne Seymour sat down to make her last will a year later, they were a married couple.

NOTES

[1] John Gough Nichols, "Anne Duchess of Somerset," *The Gentleman's Magazine 23*, p. 372.

[2] Marjorie Blatcher (ed.), *The Seymour Papers 1532-1686*, p. 185.

[3] John Gough Nichols, *The Progresses and Public Processions of Queen Elizabeth*, p. 133.

[4] John Gough Nichols, "Anne Duchess of Somerset," *The Gentleman's Magazine 23*, p. 380.

[5] Graham Bathe and Andrew Douglas, "Forging alliances: the Life of Edward Seymour, Earl of Hertford, and his commissioning of the Great Illuminated Roll Pedigree of the Seymours and monumental tombs in Wiltshire and Westminster" in *The Wiltshire Archaeological and Natural History Magazine, Volume 105 (2012)*, p. 214.

[6] Marjorie Blatcher (ed.), *The Seymour Papers 1532-1686*, p. 196.
[7] Whether she sustained her loss through miscarriage, stillbirth or any other way is unknown. Hertford, who had the letter in his possession, wrote: "Copy of the boys' letters to my sister Mary upon her distress and loss of her child". Marjorie Blatcher (ed.), *The Seymour Papers 1532-1686*, p. 144.
[8] Ibid., p. 191.
[9] Frances's father was the half brother of Queen Elizabeth's maternal grandmother, Elizabeth Boleyn.
[10] Marjorie Blatcher (ed.), *The Seymour Papers 1532-1686*, p. 149.
[11] Ibid., p. 193.
[12] Ibid., p. 190.
[13] John Gough Nichols, "Anne Duchess of Somerset," *The Gentleman's Magazine 23*, p. 377.
[14] John Edward Jackson, *Wulfhall and the Seymours*, p. 44.
[15] *Calendar of the Manuscripts of the Most Hon. the Marquess of Salisbury*, p. 520.
[16] Marjorie Blatcher (ed.), *The Seymour Papers 1532-1686*, p. 149, p. 155
[17] Ibid., p. 158.
[18] Ibid., p. 160.
[19] Ibid., p. 160.

CHAPTER 15: SETTING ALL THINGS IN ORDER

On 14 July 1586, Anne Seymour, Duchess of Somerset, composed her last will. She made her eldest son, the Earl of Hertford, her chief executor, bequeathing him "and his heirs forever" her house at Cannon Row, Westminster, "with the household and furniture thereof". She also willed him a glass of crystal adorned with gold, a basin and ewer—all gilt plaited, a pair of gilt pots, a pair of newly bought flagons, three gilt trenchers, a spoon of gold and four other spoons in "antique fashion". She also stipulated:

"Item: I give him two of the fairest gilt bowls with covers, a salt of crystal, and my best chain of great pearls with long beads of gold in between, a fair jewel of diamonds, and a great pearl worth by estimation about £30."

Frances, "his wife, my daughter of Hertford", received "a fair tablet to wear with antique work of one side and a row of diamonds on the other side", as well as "a clock of gold work worth about £30". Anne's second-oldest son received:

"Item, I give to my son the Lord Henry Seymour xiij hundred pounds of lawful English money, over and above the vij hundred I have already given him towards the payment of his debts. Item, I give him a fair jewel of an egret with divers stones. Item, I give him ij bowls of silver and gilt, with ewers, and a basin and ewer of silver."

Only three of Anne's daughters were alive at the time when she composed her last will: Anne, Mary and Elizabeth. Anne, widow of John Dudley the younger, second Earl of Warwick, remarried to Sir Edward Unton of Farrington but was styled as Countess of Warwick until her death. At some point in 1566, she was declared a "lunatic"—a mentally ill person. What caused her to decline into mental illness is unknown, but it is believed she experienced lucid intervals.[1] The duchess didn't include her eldest daughter in her last will. Mary, married to Sir Andrew Rogers, received "all my lease and term of years in the manner and farm of Ashford, in the county of Middlesex", as well as a fair share of jewels: a carcanet made of three hundred pearls, two ropes of pearls "in number about ij thousand", a lace with small pearl, a jewel of jacinth, round with small pearl, a couple of bowls with covers, a spice box of silver with the furniture of it, a silver-and-gilt ladle, and "my saddle embroidered with black velvet". Elizabeth, married to Sir Richard Knightley, received "a great chain of pearl with trueloves, a jewel of a balas, two great standing cups of silver and gilt, a jug of stone fairly dressed with silver and gilt, and a skillet of silver".

Anne's grandsons, Beauchamp and Thomas, received their portions of the duchess's wealth. Beauchamp received "two hundred pounds of lawful English money and a chain of pearl and gold with friar's knots, the gold by estimation worth about £80". His wife, Honora, was given "a book of gold kept in green purse and a pair of bracelets without stones". Thomas, as yet unmarried, received £100 and a chain worth about £60. The duchess's sons-in-law, Andrew Rogers and Richard Knightley, received a chain of gold black" and "one of my rings that had the best diamonds" respectively.

Among other members of her family, Anne mentioned "my goddaughter Anne Knightley", who received £50 and "a rope of small pearl, in number about a thousand". John and Michael Stanhope, the duchess's nephews (sons of her executed half brother) were also included. John received £40 "he owned me" while Michael received "a pillar of gold with eight diamonds" Jane Seymour, nee Poyntz, wife of Sir John Seymour, the illegitimate brother of the duchess's first husband, was listed among the servants and received a large sum of £100. This Jane Seymour served the duchess faithfully and was at her bedside when she died.

Anne possessed a vast amount of jewellery, clothing, plate and linen, too much to include all of them individually in the will, so she stipulated that:

"Item: All the rest of my plate not given before I give to my four children, equally to be divided between them.

Item: I give a coffer of sheets and pillowberes and a case standard with fine white napery to my two daughters, equally to be divided.

Item: I give to the same my two daughters my apparel, equally also to be divided."

As was customary among the upper classes, Anne made generous bequests to her servants. They received money in cash, and annuities were to be paid to them to the rest of their lives by the duchess's executor, Hertford. Some servants, like William Dickinson, Richard Saunders, Richard

Lanckeshire, John Trodde and "mother Gardener", were mentioned by name. Other male servants were mentioned collectively: "I give to all the rest of my gentlemen, yeomen, and grooms, and others in ordinary, a year's wages." Anne also mentioned her female servants:

"Item: I give to Margaret Ashurst all my wearing linen, which is in her keeping, and a new black satin gown.

Item: I give to Anne Jones 40 shillings.

Item: I give to Mrs Ansley a gown of wrought velvet furred thorough with coney.

Item: I give to Jane Seymour £100 of lawful English money."

Anne stipulated that:

"The rest of all my lands, tenements, rents, plate, jewels, with other goods, leases, chattels, horses, mares, geldings, oxen, sheep, and all other stock and store, together with all money, debts, now or hereafter due, by bond, covenant, or otherwise, my debts and legacies being paid, I give to my son the Earle of Hertford, whom I make and appoint my sole executor, to see my debts paid and my legacies faithfully performed, and my funerals discharged according to this my last will and testament. In witness whereof, to this my last will and testament, I have subscribed my name with mine own hand, and put my seal this day and year abovesaid."[2]

The document, witnessed by her preacher, William Clarke, and two physicians, Dr Penny and Dr Muffit, was signed by the duchess and placed in her "chief jewel chest, laid up among her chief jewels".

On 7 April 1587, Queen Elizabeth sent Sir Thomas Gorges to Hanworth to persuade the duchess to name her son Henry as her chief executor. Anne agreed that "my last will is Her Majesty's will" and sent the Queen a ring to confirm her promise. The next day Hertford came to his mother's bedside and addressed the following speech to her:

"I understand that Sir Thomas Gorges hath been with your Grace from the Queen's Majesty, and I cannot learn what the matter is, and I pray God that both Her Majesty, your Grace, and myself are not abused by him; but if it be to take away any trust reposed upon me, and to lay it upon my brother Harry, I beseech your Grace to let me understand it, and I shall be very contented withal."

Anne only replied, "No, no son, there is no such matter". She clearly had no wish to appoint Henry as her executor. Perhaps she was still angry about "some unnatural and unjust dealing used by Henry towards me" in 1581. It's equally possible that she disapproved of his wife, Jane Percy, who came from a recusant Catholic family.

On Good Friday of 1587, Anne's physician, Dr Muffit, "seeing her Grace to be very weak, and more likely to die than to live, did not only advertise [inform] her Grace of her weakness, but also earnestly moved her to set all things in order". Dr Muffit witnessed Anne's meeting with Sir Thomas Gorges and knew about her oral promise to the Queen. He wanted the duchess to change her last will accordingly with the promise she made Elizabeth, so that "all controversy between her children might be cut away after her decease". "No, no, what needs it?" was Anne's reply. Dr Muffit asked plainly: "Is it then your Grace's pleasure to do for my Lord Harry accordingly to your Grace's message sent unto her Majesty by Sir Thomas Gorges?" Anne replied in affirmative ("yea, yea") but died on 16 April 1587 before she could make changes to her will.[3]

Anne was buried in Westminster Abbey, and Queen Elizabeth made sure that her funeral was splendid:

"At the sumptuous and stately funerals of the last Anne duchesse of Somerset, which were performed by the right honourable Edward Earle of Hertford her executor, anno 1587, there was a portraiture of the same duchesse made in robes of her estate, with a coronal to a duchesse, and the same representation bore under a canopy; and all the other ceremonies accomplished; and because there was no duchesse to assist thereat, the Queen's Majesty gave her royal consent that the Countess of Hertford his wife should have all honour done to her after that estate during the funeral. As by warrant directed to me under Her Majesty's hand appears."[4]

An impressive tomb erected by Hertford in his beloved mother's memory still stands in the Chapel of St. Nicholas. The epitaph reads:

"Heare lieth entombed the noble duchesse of Somerset, Anne, deere spouse unto the renowned prince Edward Duke of Somerset, Earle of Hertford, Viscount Beauchampe and Baron Seymour, Compaignon [Companion] of the most famous knightly Order of the Garter: uncle to King Edward the Sixth, Gouvernor of His Roial Person and most worthie Protector of all his realmes, dominions, and subiectes: Leiutenant Generall of all his armies: threasoror and Erle Marschall of England, Gouvernor and capitayne of the Isles of Guernsey and Jersey: under whose prosperous conduct, glorious victory hath ben so often and so fortunatly obteyned over the Scottes, vanquished at Edinburgh, Leth [Leith], and Musselborough Field.

A princesse discended of noble lignage, beinge daughter of the worthie knight Sr Edward Stanhope, by Elizabeth his wyfe that was daughter of Sr Foulke Bourghchier Lord Fitzwarin, from whome our moderne earles of Bathe ar spronge, sonne was he unto Willm. Lord Fitzwarin, that was brother to Henry, Earle of Essex and Ihon [John] Lord Berners: whome Willm. their sire sometyme Earle of Ev in Normandy, begat Anne the sole heire of Thomas of Woodstock, Duke of Gloucester, yonger sonne to the mighty Prince, Kinge Edward the Third, and of his wyfe Aleanore, coheire unto the tenth Humphrey De Bohun that was Erle of Hereford, Essex and Northampton, High Constable of England.

Many children bare this lady unto her Lord, of either sort: to witte Edward, Erle of Hertford, Henry, and a younger Edward: Anne, Countesse of Warwike, Margaret, Jane, Mary, Katherine, and Elizabeth. And with firme faith in Christ in most mylde maner renred [rendered] she this life at XC yeres of age on Easter day, the sixtenth of Aprill Anno.M.CCCCC.LXXXVII.

The Erle of Hertford, Edward her eldest sonne, in this dolefull dutie carefull and diligent, doth consecrate this monument to his deere parent: not for her honor wherewith lyvinge she did abounde and nowe departed flourisheth: but for the dutifull love he beareth her, and for his laste testification therof."[5]

Hertford was finally reinstated to full glory in 1591 when Queen Elizabeth visited his estate at Elvetham during one of her royal progresses. He was in trouble four years later when he petitioned to have his first marriage proclaimed valid, thus legitimising his sons. The Queen was wary of Hertford's suit and locked him up in the Tower of London yet again. His wife, Frances, heard rumours that this time Hertford would not emerge from prison alive, and was deeply distressed. Queen Elizabeth, however, wrote a letter to her "good Francke", assuring her that no matter what Hertford did, she would never execute him. Elizabeth firmly believed that Hertford's actions demonstrated his "lewd and proud contempt" but assured Frances that his crimes would not reflect badly on her since she was "ignorant of all the causes". The Queen's letter is a testament to her strong friendship with Frances, a friendship that did not diminish even after Frances married Herford:

"It is far from our desire to pick out faults in such as he; being slow to rigour towards the meanest, we will use no more severity than is requisite for others' caution in like cases, and than shall stand with honour and necessity. Your Ladyship will quickly judge when you understand it, that his offence can have no colour of imputation on you, and you will not be one jot the less esteemed for any faults of his."[6]

Elizabeth imposed a staggering fine of £5,000. Already heavily in debt, Hertford never tried to legitimise his first marriage again.

As the Virgin Queen's reign was heading towards its end and Elizabeth still refused to name her heir, several candidates were said to be her likely successors. Among the twelve possible candidates for the throne, there was James VI of Scotland, son of the executed Mary Stuart; Arabella Stuart, great-great-granddaughter of Henry VII; and Hertford's sons. In 1594, a book entitled *A Conference about the Next Succession to the Crown of England* was published by Robert Parons in Antwerp. It examined claims of each of the twelve candidates, Beauchamp and Thomas included.

It was clear that Beauchamp's marriage to Honora Rogers hurt his cause. Nevertheless, he was still popular among the English people, who preferred an Englishman to succeed to the throne. In 1595, Sir Michael Blount, Lieutenant of the Tower, was caught stockpiling weapons in Beauchamp's name in the event of Queen Elizabeth's death. Hertford and his son were incarcerated in the Tower but were quickly released.

On 14 May 1598, Hertford's second wife, Frances, died after a long sickness, aged forty-four, and was buried with great honours at Westminster Abbey. Her great wish of providing him with more sons was sadly unfulfilled. Two years later another tragedy befell Hertford when his younger son, Thomas, died without progeny. But the proud Hertford still entertained hope that a Seymour would succeed Queen Elizabeth and schemed to have his grandson, the younger Edward Seymour (Beauchamp's son), married to Arabella Stuart, the girl who was considered by many a strong contender to the crown. Yet it seemed clear that James VI of Scotland would be the Queen's most likely successor, and Hertford dropped his plans, informing the Queen of a message Arabella relayed to him through one of her servants.

In early 1603, Queen Elizabeth's health began to deteriorate. Aged seventy, the Queen became speechless and communicated with her prelates and courtiers only by gestures. In her final illness, she refused to take to bed, eat or accept medical help. When the Lord Admiral Charles Howard, brother of the late Frances, Countess of Hertford, was summoned to the Queen's side, he encouraged her to rest in bed instead of sitting motionlessly on the floor among her cushions with a finger constantly in her mouth. It was believed that he would be able to persuade the Queen to rest, but Elizabeth "said softly to him if he had known what she had seen in her bed he would not persuade her as he did".[7] The Lord Admiral at least managed to convince Elizabeth to eat some broth, but the Queen complained that she felt as if "tied with a chain of iron about my neck". Two of her ladies discovered a queen of hearts playing card "with an iron nail knocked through the head of it" underneath Elizabeth's chair. The ladies were afraid to remove the card, "thinking it to be some witchcraft".[8] In reality, it was not witchcraft that killed Elizabeth, as the Queen was troubled with a "sore throat" as well as "heat in her breasts and dryness in her mouth and tongue" caused by a combination of tonsillitis and the flu.[9]

Hertford took a keen interest in the Queen's last illness, as evidenced by his miscellaneous expenses. Between January and March, he paid for "my journeys to Richmond during the Queen's sickness".[10] Like many of his contemporaries, Hertford expected that civil war would break out upon Elizabeth's death. On 23 March, the members of the Privy Council made one last attempt to ask the Queen, now on her deathbed, if she would nominate an heir. Since Elizabeth "spoke very seldom having then a sore throat", her councillors suggested that she raise her finger when they named the successor whom she accepted. When they named James VI of Scotland, she "never stirred", but when they asked whether Lord Beauchamp, Hertford's son, was acceptable, she gathered her last ounces of strength and said, "I will have no rascal's son in my seat but one worthy to be a King".[11] These were her last words.

In the end, King James VI ascended the English throne as James I, but he feared the Seymours and never lifted their stain of illegitimacy despite the fact that, in 1608, Hertford had found the anonymous preacher who had married him to Katherine Grey forty-eight years earlier.

Edward Seymour, Viscount Beauchamp, died in 1612, predeceasing his father. His legacy lived on in two sons he had with Honora: William and Francis.[12] In 1610, William continued the family tradition and secretly married Lady Arabella Stuart, the King's kinswoman. James strongly disapproved of the marriage as the union of two potential Tudor pretenders to the throne and locked the couple in the Tower of London. William and Arabella planned their escape, but in the end only William made it safely out of the Tower and to France, whereas Arabella, detained by foul weather, was rearrested. She died in the Tower in 1615.

Hertford himself remarried after his second wife's death. His new wife was also named Frances Howard. Born in 1578, she was the daughter of Thomas Howard, 1st Viscount Howard of Bindon, and his wife, Mabel Burton, and, more famously, a granddaughter of Thomas Howard, 3rd Duke of Norfolk. Rising from rags to riches, this Frances Seymour would outlive her ageing husband and become one of the celebrated beauties of the Jacobean court.

Edward Seymour, Earl of Hertford, died on 6 April 1621 at the astonishing age of eighty-two. It was his grandson William who inherited the earldom of Hertford. Twenty years later William was created Marquis of Hertford and in 1660 received the Lord Protector's dukedom of Somerset, becoming the second Duke of Somerset of the Seymour family. It is often claimed that it was William who erected a splendid tomb for his grandparents, Hertford and Katherine Grey, at Salisbury Cathedral. However, it has been recently proposed by Graham Bathe and Andrew Douglas that the tomb was erected on Hertford's orders. William showed scant interest in funeral monuments and was not close to his grandfather, whereas Hertford ordered four monuments for the members of his family: Sir John Seymour (his grandfather), Jane Seymour (his sister), Anne Seymour (his mother) and Frances Seymour (his second wife). Although the Salisbury monument was not constructed until after Hertford's death, it is believed that the inscriptions were drafted during his lifetime.

It is often popularly assumed that Katherine Grey was disinterred from her humble grave in Yoxford, Suffolk, and reinterred at Salisbury Cathedral, where she is now buried with her husband. Bathe and Douglas pointed out, however, that whereas Hertford is certainly buried at Salisbury, there is no evidence that Katherine is buried with him.[13] Whatever the truth of the matter, the monument at Salisbury Cathedral still stands today, one of the five Seymour funeral monuments built by the Earl of Hertford, a reminder of a family that brushed with treason on so many occasions.

Although Hertford proudly proclaimed himself to be "son of the renowned Prince Edward Duke of Somerset", his father lies buried beneath the pavement at the Chapel of St Peter ad Vincula in the Tower of London. During the restoration of the chapel in 1876, skeletal remains of several bodies were found, examined and reburied. Somerset was originally buried "on the north side of the choir of St Peter's".[14] Ironically, he was buried close to the Duke of Northumberland, his mortal enemy, the man who before his own execution confessed that he had "procured his [Somerset's] death unjustly" and that "nothing had pressed so injuriously upon his conscience as the fraudulent scheme against the Duke of Somerset which would never have come to pass without his authority and favour".[15] There they were, "before the high altar in St Peter's church, two Dukes between two Queens, to wit, the Duke of Somerset and the Duke of Northumberland, between Queen Anne and Queen Katherine, all four beheaded".[16]

NOTES

[1] John Gough Nichols, *The Unton Inventories*, p. xliv.
[2] John Gough Nichols, "Anne Duchess of Somerset," *The Gentleman's Magazine 23*, pp. 375-380.
[3] Ibid.
[4] Thomas Hearne, *A Collection of Curious Discourses Written by Eminent Antiquaries Upon Several Heads in Our English Antiquities*, Volume 1, p. 204.
[5] http://www.westminster-abbey.org/our-history/people/anne-stanhope,-duchess-of-somerset
[6] *Calendar of State Papers: Edward VI, Mary, Elizabeth and James I. 1547-1625,* Volume 4, pp. 121-122.
[7] Henry Clifford, *The Life of Jane Dormer, Duchess of Feria*, p. 99.
[8] Ibid.
[9] Frederick Chamberlin, *The Private Character of Queen Elizabeth,* p. 75. In her book *After Elizabeth: The Rise of James of Scotland and the Struggle for the Throne of England* (p. 55), historian Leanda de Lisle suggested that the Queen suffered from Ludwig's angina.
[10] Marjorie Blatcher (ed.), *The Seymour Papers 1532-1686*, p. 205.
[11] Catherine Loomis, *Elizabeth Southwell's Manuscript Account of the Death of Queen Elizabeth I*, p. 485.
[12] His eldest son, Edward, died.
[13] Graham Bathe and Andrew Douglas, "Forging alliances: the Life of Edward Seymour, Earl of Hertford, and his commissioning of the Great Illuminated Roll Pedigree of the Seymours and monumental tombs in Wiltshire and Westminster" in *The Wiltshire Archaeological and Natural History Magazine, Volume 105 (2012)*, p. 214.
[14] *The Diary of Henry Machyn*, p. 14.
[15] D. E. Hoak, *The King's Council in the Reign of Edward VI,* p. 74.
[16] Doyne C. Bell, *Notices of the Historic Persons Buried in the Chapel of St. Peter Ad Vincula*, p. 51.

Appendix 1: When was Anne Seymour born?

Anne Seymour's birthdate was not recorded. According to an inscription on her tomb, erected by her eldest son, she was ninety years old when she died in 1587, setting her birthdate in the year 1497. Historian William Camden, writing the first ever biography of Queen Elizabeth I in the seventeenth century, also asserted that Anne died "being ninety years of age", a remarkable achievement in an era when diseases and plagues were rampant.[1] However, today historians tend to believe that Anne was born in 1510, and this date tallies well with her childbearing history.

NOTES

[1] William Camden, *The History of the Most Renowned and Victorious Princess Elizabeth Late Queen of England*, p. 401.

Appendix 2: The Children of Anne and Edward Seymour

Anne and Edward Seymour had a large family. They married before 9 March 1535, and Anne embarked on childbearing soon afterwards. According to an inscription on Anne's tomb, the couple had nine children: Edward, Earl of Hertford; Henry; a younger Edward; Anne, Countess of Warwick; Margaret, Jane, Mary, Katherine and Elizabeth. Since Anne's tomb was erected by her eldest son, Hertford, it provides solid evidence, but, as becomes clear after extensive research into the duchess's childbearing, the children mentioned on the tomb are those who survived into adulthood. Those who died young were not mentioned.

The best evidence of how many children Anne and Edward had comes from a letter written by Thomas Norton to John Calvin on 13 November 1553. Norton, secretary to the Duke of Somerset, knew exactly how many children his "late master" had. Since Calvin corresponded with the duchess and her eldest daughter, Anne, he was interested in what happened to the Seymour children after their father's execution in 1552. Norton first mentioned the girls in the order of their birth:

"With respect to their maintenance, the following provision was made. The eldest daughter Anne, with whom you have corresponded, has been married nearly three years to the earl of Warwick, son and heir to the duke of Northumberland, and is happily and honourably settled. The other four, Margaret, Jane, Maria, and Catharine, are unmarried, and committed by the Council to the care of their aunt, the widow of the lord Cromwell, to whom four hundred marks are yearly paid by the King for their maintenance, according to the act of Parliament. Each mark is worth thirteen shillings and fourpence. The youngest daughter, Elizabeth, who is now in her second year, is with her aunt Smith, who lost her husband about four months since, and to whom in like manner a hundred marks are yearly assigned for her support."[1]

The exact dates of their births were not always recorded in the sources but are possible to detect. Anne, the eldest daughter and the first child of Anne and Edward's, was born before 1537. The baby whose christening was recorded on 22 February 1537 was a girl named Jane, doubtless after Queen Jane Seymour, who stood as one of two godmothers, the second being the Lady Mary:

"Linen cloth: Paid for 3 ells of Holland at 20d to line font the day of christening of mistress Jane and after delivered to Roger Cotton, Yeoman of the Vellum [?] for a cupboard cloth 22 February. 5s."[2]

The baby Jane visited Lady Mary in November 1537 since Mary's Privy Purse expenses recorded a payment "to the nurse of my Lady of Hertford's coming with one of her daughters, my Lady's Grace being godmother to the same".[3] However, an inventory of household furniture, plate and supplies compiled between 1538 and 1547 clarifies that in 1539-40 Anne and Edward had two daughters, as it mentions "nursery furniture including the beds of Lady Anne, Lady Margaret and the nurse".[4] The baby Jane born in 1537 must have died early in her childhood as no further mention of her is made in the existing Seymour household accounts. The name was, however, dear to Anne and Edward, who named another of their daughters, born in 1541, Jane.

Three of Anne's six daughters were alive at the time she composed her last will in 1586. Anne, Countess of Warwick, was mentally ill; she outlived her mother and died in 1588. Mary was married to Sir Andrew Rogers, and Elizabeth, the youngest daughter, to Sir Richard Knightley.

Others predeceased their mother. Jane died on 19 March 1560; the monument erected in her memory by Hertford settles the year of her birth as 1541 since it specifies that she "departed this lyfe in her virginite at ye age of ninteen yeares".[5] The deaths of Margaret and Katherine were not recorded. Three Seymour sisters—Mary, Katherine and Elizabeth—were alive and unmarried in 1563 since their brother Hertford paid £20 for their upkeep.[6] Katherine may have been born in August 1544 and named after Queen Katherine Parr, Henry VIII's wife at the time. This would explain why the Queen attended the christening in person (perhaps as one of the godmothers) as recorded in her payments:

"Kyrton, master of the barge, for serving the Queen with the close barge to the earl of Harford's [sic] house and the lady Harbert from Thisleworth to Westm., 33s. 8d.; also attending the Queen with the barges at her going to the christening of the earl of Hartford's child and lying one night at Richmond, 6l. 8s. 8d."[7]

Thomas Norton's letter also gives detailed information as to Anne and Edward's sons:

"To Edward, his [the Duke of Somerset's] son and heir, thirteen years old, and as it were the living image of his father, out of the estates which yielded annually to his father [blank] thousand pounds of our money, each of which is equivalent to four golden crowns, as they call them, there is reserved, by the same act of Parliament, about two thousand four hundred pounds, more or less. The surplus, with all the personalty, was paid, as is wont, into the exchequer. He, with his two brothers, Henry and Edward, the latter five years old, and the other twelve, is with the lord treasurer of England. They are wards of the King, to whom, as long as they are under age, belongs the guardianship of noble orphans, and also the use, enjoyment, and management of their estates."[8]

It is somewhat confusing that two of the Seymour sons were christened Edward (three, if the Duke of Somerset's son by his first wife is to be taken into consideration). The elder Edward, who became his father's heir and the Earl of Hertford, was born on 22 May 1539.[9] The younger Edward, who was five years old in 1553, was born in 1548, as evidenced by a letter of Edward VI's page John Fowler to Thomas Seymour on 18 July 1548:

"My Lady of Somerset is brought to bed of a goodly boy, thanks be it to God; and, I trust in almighty God, the Queen's Grace [Katherine Parr] shall have another."[10]

Henry, twelve in 1553, was born in 1541. Another Henry, who died at some point during his childhood, was born on 12 March 1538 as is evidenced by an entry in the following inventory item:

"Paid in reward to the lord of the wardrobe with the king for hanging of the chapel and porch at Beauchamp place for the christening of my lord's son, called Henry [some damage here] Lord Beauchamp, 14 March, who was born the 12 day of the same month at or between 4 and five of the clock in the forenoon. 20 s."[11]

His birth was also recorded in the King's payments since Henry VIII laid out a handsome sum for "a certain cup given at the christening of the earl of Hertford's son".[12]

When Anne Seymour composed her last will, two of her sons were still alive: Hertford and the younger Henry. The younger Edward predeceased his mother, as in 1581 Hertford stated that a "villain" priest named Braddock refused to "bury my brother Edward".[13]

Based on the abovementioned evidence, it appears that Anne and Edward Seymour had eleven children, two of whom died during their childhood. Among them were two Janes, two Edwards and two Henrys. Five were still alive when Anne died in 1587: Hertford, Henry, Anne, Mary and Elizabeth.

NOTES

[1] Hastings Robinson, *Original Letters Relative to the English Reformation*, Volume 1, p. 342.
[2] Sarah Morris, Natalie Grueninger, *In the Footsteps of the Six Wives of Henry VIII*, p. 191.
[3] Frederic Madden, *Privy Purse Expenses of the Princess Mary*, p. 46.
[4] Marjorie Blatcher (ed.), *The Seymour Papers 1532-1686*, p. 120.
[5] http://www.westminster-abbey.org/our-history/people/anne-stanhope,-duchess-of-somerset
[6] Marjorie Blatcher (ed.), *The Seymour Papers 1532-1686*, p. 178.
[7] *Letters and Papers, Henry VIII*, Volume 19 Part 2, n. 688.
[8] Hastings Robinson, *Original Letters Relative to the English Reformation*, Volume 1, p. 342.
[9] Muriel St Clare Byrne, *The Lisle Letters*, Volume 5, pp. 493, 508.
[10] Janel Mueller, *Katherine Parr: Complete Works and Correspondence*, p. 173.
[11] Sarah Morris, Natalie Grueninger, *In the Footsteps of the Six Wives of Henry VIII*, p. 191.
[12] *Letters and Papers, Henry VIII*, Volume 13 Part 2, n. 1280 (f. 17).
[13] Marjorie Blatcher (ed.), *The Seymour Papers 1532-1686*, p. 193.

Picture Section

The Seymours

Plate 1: Anne Seymour, nee Stanhope, Duchess of Somerset. This drawing of the original portrait, now lost, shows the duchess in her prime, proudly holding a locket with a miniature of her husband.

Plate 2: Portrait of Edward Seymour as Earl of Hertford. The Latin inscription on either side of his head reads: "E(dwardus) SE(ymour) C(omes) HER(tfordiensis)" ("Edward Seymour, Earl of Hertford"). He became Lord Protector and Duke of Somerset at the commencement of Edward VI's reign. He was executed in 1552.

Plate 3: Anne Seymour, Duchess of Somerset as a widow: This portrait's current whereabouts are unknown, but the coat of arms suggests this is indeed Anne.

Plate 4: Somerset Place from the Panorama of London, Westminster and Southwark in the 1540s: Somerset Place was the lavish ducal palace of Edward and Anne Seymour, the first example of Italianate style of building in England. In the words of the imperial ambassador, the Duke of Somerset appeared to have had "no care but to build houses for himself and deliver the realm to the enemy".

Plate 5: Somerset Place as it appeared in the 16th century: The site was still unfinished when Edward Seymour was executed in 1552. Lady Elizabeth, later Queen, used it as her London residence.

Plate 6: Thomas Seymour, Baron Seymour of Sudeley: Handsome and ambitious younger brother of Edward, Duke of Somerset, Thomas married Katherine Parr soon after Henry VIII's death and hoped to win custody of his royal nephew. He was executed for treason in 1549.

Plate 7: Jane Seymour as Queen of England: Sister of Edward and Thomas Seymour, she became Henry VIII's wife on 30 May 1536, eleven days after her predecessor, Anne Boleyn, was executed on trumped-up charges of treason and adultery. She died in 1537 of postnatal complications.

Plate 8: Prince Edward: Jane Seymour gave birth to her only child, Henry VIII's longed-for male heir, on 12 October 1537. Here he is depicted as a fifteen-month-old child.

Plate 9: King Edward VI: Edward succeeded his father in 1547. Jehan Scheyfve, imperial ambassador, described him as a "lad of quick, ready and well-developed mind; remarkably so for his age". Edward was handsome and learned and was slowly becoming ready to assume power on his own. His premature death on 6 July 1553 shocked the nation.

Plate 10: Katherine Seymour, Countess of Hertford: Lady Jane Grey's younger sister, Katherine, fell in love with Edward Seymour, Earl of Hertford, son of the executed Duke of Somerset. Katherine was Queen Elizabeth's heiress under Henry VIII's will, but the Queen never acknowledged Katherine as such. Katherine's secret marriage to Hertford marked her as Queen Elizabeth's greatest enemy and rival. She died under house arrest in 1568, committing suicide by starvation.

Plate 11: Edward Seymour, Earl of Hertford: The eldest surviving son of Anne and Edward Seymour, Hertford was said to have been "the living image of his father". His marriage to Katherine Grey, sister of the executed Lady Jane, made him unpopular with Queen Elizabeth.

The Dudleys

Plate 12: John Dudley, Duke of Northumberland: Grandest enemy of Edward Seymour, Duke of Somerset, he abolished the title of Lord Protector and became Lord President of the Privy Council. He was executed by Queen Mary in 1553 after his daughter-in-law, Lady Jane Grey, lost her throne.

Plate 13: Robert Dudley, Earl of Leicester: One of John's sons, he rose high during the reign of Queen Elizabeth.

Plate 14: Lady Jane Grey: On his deathbed, fifteen-year-old Edward VI made his last will, wherein he named his Protestant cousin Lady Jane Grey heiress to his throne. She was proclaimed Queen on 10 July 1553. Her reign was brief and ended with Mary Tudor winning her throne on 19 July. Many believed that since Lady Jane was married to Northumberland's son Guildford Dudley, Northumberland would be de facto king.

The Parrs

Plate 15: Katherine Parr as Queen of England: Katherine was Henry VIII's sixth and final wife. She married Thomas Seymour in the spring of 1547 with unseemly haste. Their marriage enraged Edward and Anne Seymour.

Plate 16: William Parr, Marquis of Northampton: Katherine Parr's brother. His first marriage to Anne Bourchier was a disaster; Anne eloped with her lover and bore him two children. In the 1540s, William fell in love with Elisabeth Brooke, daughter of George Brooke, 9th Baron Cobham. He married her in 1548.

Plate 17: Elisabeth Parr, nee Brooke, Marchioness of Northampton: Daughter of George Brooke, 9th Baron Cobham and Anne Braye. She started her career at court as Katherine Parr's maid of honour. She became a great favourite of Queen Elizabeth. The medal dates to 1562.

Plate 18: The Cobham family portrait: The painting, commissioned in 1567, depicts William Brooke, 10th Baron Cobham, with his wife, Frances, and six of their small children. Elisabeth Parr is believed to be one of the two depicted women—which one remains a matter of dispute among historians.

Plate 19: Elisabeth Parr and one of the two women from the Cobham family portrait: The only undisputable likeness of Elisabeth Parr is the medal dating to 1562. This sitter from the Cobham family portrait shares similar traits with Elisabeth in the medal.

SELECTED BIBLIOGRAPHY

Printed primary sources

Ascham, R. *The Whole Works of Roger Ascham.* John Russel Smith, 1865.

Bietenholz, P.G. *The Correspondence of Erasmus: Letters 842-992 (1518-1519).* University of Toronto Press, 1982.

Blatcher, M. *Seymour Papers 1532-1686*. H.M.S.O, 1968.

Brewer, J.S. & Gairdner, J., eds. *Calendar of State Papers, Spain.* Institute of Historical Research (1862-1932).

Brewer, J.S. & Gairdner, J., eds. *Letters and Papers, Foreign and Domestic, of the Reign of Henry VIII.* 28 Volumes. Institute of Historical Research (1862-1932).

Brigden, S. ed. *The Letters of Richard Scudamore to Sir Philip Hoby, September 1549-March 1555*. Camden Miscellany, xxx, (Camden Soc. 4th ser. 39, 1990).

Camden, W. *The History of the Most Renowned and Victorious Princess Elizabeth Late Queen of England*. Flesher, 1688.

Clifford, H. *The Life of Jane Dormer, Duchess of Feria.* Burns & Oates, 1887.

Dowling, M., ed. *William Latymer's Cronickille of Anne Bulleyne*. Camden Miscellany, xxx (Camden Soc. 4th ser. 39, 1990).

Ellis, H. *Original Letters Illustrative of English History*, Volume 2. (2nd series). Harding and Lepard, 1827.

Everett Wood, A. *Letters of Royal and Illustrious Ladies of Great Britain, Three Volumes.* London: H. Colburn, 1846.

Foxe, J. *The Actes and Monuments of the Church*. Hobart Seymour, ed. M. Robert Carter & Brothers, 1855.

Gough Nichols, J. *The Chronicle of Queen Jane and of Two Years of Queen Mary.* Camden Society, 1850.

Gough Nichols, J. *The Literary Remains of Edward the Sixth. Edited From His Autograph Manuscripts, With Historical Notes and a Biographical Memoir.* J.B. Nichols, 1859.

Hall, E. *Hall's Chronicle.* J. Johnson, 1809.

Harris, N. *The Literary Remains of Lady Jane Grey: With a Memoir of Her Life*. Harding, Triphook, and Lepard, 1825.

Haynes, S. *A Collection of State Papers: relating to Affairs In the Reigns of King Henry VIII, King Edward VI, Queen Mary and Queen Elizabeth: From the Year 1542 to 1570*. Bowyer, 1740.

Leland, J. *Joannis Lelandi antiquarii de rebus britannicis collectanea.* Richardson, 1770.

Madden, F. *Privy Purse Expenses of the Princess Mary, Daughter of King Henry the Eighth, Afterwards Queen Mary: With a Memoir of the Princess, and Notes*. William Pickering, 1831.

Mueller, J., ed. *Katherine Parr: Complete Works and Correspondence*. University of Chicago Press, 2011.

Sander, N. *Rise and Growth of the Anglican Schism*. Burns and Oates, 1877.

Sharp Hume, M.A. *Chronicle of King Henry VIII of England*. George Bell and Sons, 1889.

St Clare Byrne, M., ed. *The Lisle Letters*. Six Volumes. The University of Chicago Press, 1981.

Wriothesley, C. *A Chronicle of England During the Reigns of the Tudors, from A.D. 1485 to 1559*. Two Volumes. Camden Society, 1875.

Secondary sources

Alford, S. *Kingship and Politics in the Reign of Edward VI.* Cambridge University Press, 2008.

Bell, D.C. *Notices of the Historic Persons Buried in the Chapel of St. Peter Ad Vincula in the Tower of London, with an Account of the Discovery of the Supposed Remains of Queen Anne Boleyn*. J. Murray, 1877.

Bernard, G.W. *Anne Boleyn: Fatal Attractions.* Yale University Press, 2010.

Bernard, G.W. *The King's Reformation*. Yale University Press, 2007.

Borman, T. *Elizabeth's Women: The Hidden Story of the Virgin Queen.* Vintage, 2010.

Bradford, C.A. *Helena, Marchioness of Northampton*. G. Allen & Unwin Limited, 1936.

Chamberlin, F. *The Private Character of Queen Elizabeth.* Dodd Mead & Company, 1922.

Childs, J. *Henry VIII's Last Victim: The Life and Times of Henry Howard, Earl of Surrey.* Thomas Dunne Books, 2007.

Collins, A. *Letters and Memorials of State*. Volume 2. T. Osborne, 1746.

De Lisle, L. *After Elizabeth: The Rise of James of Scotland and the Struggle for the Throne of England.* Ballantine Books, 2007.

De Lisle, L. *The Sisters Who Would Be Queen: The Tragedy of Mary, Katherine and Lady Jane Grey*. HarperPress, 2010.

Doran, S. *Elizabeth I and Her Circle*. Oxford University Press, 2015.

Evans, V.S. *Ladies-in-Waiting: Women Who Served at the Tudor Court.* CreateSpace, 2014.

Fox, J. *Jane Boleyn: The True Story of the Infamous Lady Rochford*. Ballantine Books, 2009.

Fraser Tytler, P. *England under the Reigns of Edward VI and Mary*. Richard Bentley, 1839.

Friedmann, P. *Anne Boleyn: A Chapter of English History, 1527-1536*. Macmillan and Co., 1884.

Furdel Lane, E. *The Royal Doctors, 1485-1714: Medical Personnel at the Tudor and Stuart Courts.* University of Rochester Press, 2001.

Gough Nichols, J. "Anne Duchess of Somerset." *The Gentleman's Magazine 23* (1845): 371-381.

Graham-Matheson, H. "Elisabeth Parr's Renaissance at the Mid-Tudor Court". *Early Modern Women.* Volume 8 (Fall 2013): 289-299.

Grueninger, N. and Morris, S. *In the Footsteps of the Six Wives of Henry VIII: The Visitor's Companion to the Palaces, Castles & Houses Associated with Henry VIII's Iconic Queens*. Amberley Publishing, 2016.

Gunn, S.J. "A Letter of Jane, Duchess of Northumberland in 1553." *English Historical Review 114* (1999): 1267–71.

Hamilton, D.B. *Shakespeare and the Politics of Protestant England*. University Press of Kentucky, 1992.

Harkrider, F.M. *Women, Reform and Community in Early Modern England.* Boydell Press, 2008.

Harris, J.B. *English Aristocratic Women, 1450-1550: Marriage and Family, Property and Careers.* Oxford University Press, 2002.

Hartweg, Ch. *Amy Robsart: A Life and Its End*. CreateSpace, 2017.

Hartweg, Ch. *John Dudley: The Life of Lady Jane Grey's Father-in-Law*. CreateSpace, 2016.

Hayward, J. *The Life and Raigne of King Edward the Sixth*. Partridge, 1630.

Head, M.D. *The Ebbs and Flows of Fortune: The Life of Thomas Howard, Third Duke of Norfolk*. University of Georgia Press, 1995.

Hutchinson, R. *The Last Days of Henry VIII: Conspiracy, Treason and Heresy at the Court of the Dying Tyrant.* Phoenix, 2006.

Ives, E. W. *The Life and Death of Anne Boleyn: The Most Happy*. Blackwell Publishing, 2010.

Ives. E. W. *Lady Jane Grey - A Tudor Mystery*. Blackwell Publishing, 2011.

Jackson, J.E. *Wulfhall and the Seymours. With an Appendix of Original Documents Discovered at Longleat*. 1874.

James, S. *Catherine Parr: Henry VIII's Last Love*. The History Press, 2010.

James, S. *The Feminine Dynamic in English Art, 1485–1603: Women as Consumers, Patrons and Painters*. Routledge, 2009.

Kelly, H.A. *The Matrimonial Trials of Henry VIII.* Wipf and Stock Publishers, 2004.

Kitchener Jordan, W. *Edward VI: The Threshold of Power: The Dominance of the Duke of Northumberland*. Belknap Press of Harvard University Press, 1970.

Klarwill, V. *Queen Elizabeth and Some Foreigners*. Bentano's, 1928.

Levin, C. and Riehl Bertolet, A. *A Biographical Encyclopedia of Early Modern Englishwomen: Exemplary Lives and Memorable Acts, 1500-1650*. Routledge, 2016.

Lipscomb, S. *1536: The Year that Changed Henry VIII*. Lion Hudson, 2009.

Loach, J. *Edward VI*. Yale University Press, 2014.

Loach, J. *Protector Somerset: A Reassessment*. Headstart History, 1994.

Loades, D. *Intrigue and Treason: The Tudor Court, 1547-1558.* Pearson, 2004.

Loades, D. *John Dudley, Duke of Northumberland 1504-1553.* Clarendon Press, 1996.

Loades, D. *Mary Tudor: A Life*. Basil Blackwell, 1989.

Loomis, C. "Elizabeth Southwell's Manuscript Account of the Death of Queen Elizabeth [with Text]". *English Literary Renaissance*, Vol. 26, No. 3, Monarchs (1996), pp. 482-509.

Lovell, M.S. *Bess of Hardwick: First Lady of Chatsworth*. Hachette UK, 2009.

Maclean, J. *The Life of Sir Thomas Seymour: Knight, Baron Seymour of Sudeley, Lord High Admiral of England and Master of the Ordnance*. J.C. Hotten, 1869.

Medici, C. "More than a Wife and Mother: Jane Dudley, the Woman Who Bequeathed a Parrot and Served Five Queens" in *Scholars and Poets Talk About Queens*, edited by C. Levin and C. Stewart-Nunez. Palgrave MacMillan, 2015.

Merriman, R.B. *Life and Letters of Thomas Cromwell*. Two Volumes. Clarendon Press, 1902.

Montrose, L. *The Subject of Elizabeth: Authority, Gender, and Representation*. University of Chicago Press, 2006.

North, J. *England's Boy King: The Diary of Edward VI, 1547-1553.* Ravenhall, 2005.

Norton, E. *Jane Seymour: Henry VIII's True Love*. Amberley, 2009.

Norton, E. *The Temptation of Elizabeth Tudor.* Head of Zeus, 2015.

Pocock, N. *Troubles Connected with the Prayer Book 1549*. Camden society, 1884.

Porter, L. *Katherine the Queen: The Remarkable Life of Katherine Parr*. Macmillan, 2010.

Powell, E. *The Travels and Life of Sir Thomas Hoby, Kt. of Bisham Abbey, Written by Himself, 1547-1564*. London : Offices of the Society, 1902.

Russell, G. *Young and Damned and Fair: The Life and Tragedy of Catherine Howard at the Court of Henry VIII*. William Collins, 2017.

Scard, M. *Edward Seymour: Lord Protector*. The History Press, 2016.

Scarisbrick, J.J. *Henry VIII*. University of California Press, 1968.

Schofield, J. *The Rise and Fall of Thomas Cromwell: Henry VIII's Most Faithful Servant*. The History Press, 2011.

Seymour, W. *Ordeal by Ambition: An English Family in the Shadow of the Tudors*. Sidgwick & Jackson, 1972.

Skidmore, Ch. *Edward VI: The Lost King of England*. W&N, 2008.
Smith, Lacey B. *Catherine Howard: The Queen Whose Adulteries Made a Fool of Henry VIII*. Amberley Publishing, 2009.

Soberton, S.B. *Golden Age Ladies: Women Who Shaped the Courts of Francis I and Henry VIII*. CreateSpace, 2016.

St Maur, R.H. *Annals of the Seymours*. Kegan Paul, 1902.

Starkey, D. *Six Wives: The Queens of Henry VIII*. Vintage, 2004.

Starkey, D. *Elizabeth: The Struggle for the Throne*. Harper Perennial, 2007.

Stone, J.M. *History of Mary I, Queen of England*. Sands & Co., 1901.

Strickland, A. *Lives of the Tudor Princesses: Including Lady Jane Gray and Her Sisters*. Longmans Green, 1868.

Strong, R. *Artists of the Tudor Court*. Victoria & Albert Museum, 1983.

Strype. J. *The Life of the Learned Sir John Cheke, Kt., First Instructor, Afterwards Secretary of State, to King Edward VI*. Clarendon Press, 1821.

Tremlett, G. *Catherine of Aragon: Henry's Spanish Queen.* Faber & Faber, 2010.

Walker, G. "Rethinking the Fall of Anne Boleyn". *The Historical Journal*, Vol. 45, No. 1 (Mar., 2002), pp. 1-29.

Warnicke, R.M. *The Rise and Fall of Anne Boleyn: Family Politics at the Court of Henry VIII.* Cambridge University Press, 1991.

Warnicke, R.M. *Wicked Women of Tudor England.* Palgrave MacMillan, 2012.

Weir, A. *The Lady in the Tower: The Fall of Anne Boleyn.* Vintage, 2010.

Weir, A. *The Six Wives of Henry VIII.* Vintage, 2007.

Whitelock, A. *Elizabeth's Bedfellows: An Intimate History of the Queen's Court.* Bloomsbury Publishing, 2013.

Whitelock, A. *Mary Tudor: England's First Queen.* Bloomsbury Publishing, 2010.

Wilkinson, J. *Katherine Howard: The Tragic Story of Henry VIII's Fifth Queen.* Hachette UK, 2016.

Williams, P. *Catherine of Aragon: The Tragic Story of Henry VIII's First Unfortunate Wife.* Amberley Publishing, 2013.

Wilson, D. *The Uncrowned Kings of England: The Black Legend of the Dudleys.* Robinson, 2005.

PhD Dissertations

Clark, A.B. Thought, word and deed in the mid-Tudor Commonwealth: Sir Thomas Smith and Sir William Cecil in the Reign of Edward VI. Portland State University, 1979.

De Witte Bowles, C. Women of the Tudor court, 1501-1568.Portland State University, 1989.

Hamilton, D. The Household of Queen Katherine Parr. University of Oxford, 1992.

Walters Schmid, S. Anne Boleyn, Lancelot de Carle, and the Uses of Documentary Evidence. Arizona State University, 2009.

Websites

http://www.british-history.ac.uk/catalogue

http://www.oxford-shakespeare.com/

https://allthingsrobertdudley.wordpress.com/

https://archive.org/

https://www.westminster-abbey.org/

Made in the USA
Las Vegas, NV
30 November 2024